SOS!

Help For Parents

Lynn Clark, Ph.D.

Illustrations by John Robb

Parents Press
Post Office Box 2180
Bowling Green, Ky. 42102-2180, U.S.A.

SOS! Help For Parents

Library of Congress Cataloging-in-Publication Data

Clark, Lynn, date.
  SOS! : help for parents.

  Bibliography: p.
  Includes index.
  1. Children- -Discipline. 2. Child rearing.
3. Timeout method. I. Title.
HQ770.4.C52   1985   649'.64   85-16950
ISBN 0-935111-16-6

Printed in the United States of America

Published by: **Parents Press**
Post Office Box 2180
Bowling Green, Ky. 42102-2180

20 19 18 17 16 15 14 13 12 11

Publisher's Note

WARNING

This book is designed to provide information in regard to the subject matter covered. It is sold with the understanding that the publisher and author are not engaged in rendering psychological, medical, or other professional services.

Rearing children is sometimes very difficult. If expert assistance is needed, seek the services of a competent professional. Chapter 22 describes how to obtain professional help.

DEDICATION

To children and those who rear them

ACKNOWLEDGEMENTS

I am especially indebted to Gerald Patterson, Rex Forehand, and their colleagues for much of this book's research and clinical foundations. Donald Baer introduced me to behavioral child management research when I was a graduate student at The University of Kansas. B.F. Skinner, for more than a half-century, has contributed fundamental research on human behavior and also kindly gave his permission to use the cartoon illustration in Chapter 22.

Gerald Patterson at the Oregon Social Learning Center and Mark Roberts at Idaho State University reviewed the manuscript. Their comments and recommendations improved the usefulness of *SOS!*

Carole Clark critiqued each of the many manuscript drafts and contributed true examples of problem behaviors and parent-child interactions. Mary Ann Kearny and Virginia Lezhnev made suggestions regarding writing style and provided encouragement.

Individuals at Western Kentucky University who contributed to *SOS!* include Patrice Nolan, Lois Layne, Clinton Layne, Harry Robe, William Pfohl, Elsie Dotson, Ned Kearny, Fred Stickle, Livingston Alexander, Carl Martray, Delbert Hayden, and James Warwick. Many graduate and undergraduate students also contributed useful comments regarding the manuscript.

Copyreading was done by Beverly Cravens. Janet Allen and Rhonda Kessinger helped type the manuscript revisions. Bettye Neblett offered valuable suggestions regarding *SOS!* and provided swift, expert typing.

CONTENTS

Section Two
BASIC SKILLS OF THE TIME-OUT METHOD

Section Three
FURTHER APPLICATIONS OF YOUR PARENTING SKILLS

"Happy together!"

INTRODUCTION

JESSICA

"I always win!"

Six-year-old Jessica was out of control. When angry, she bit her wrist till it bled, screamed and swore, hit her mother or attacked a wall or door in a fit of rage! Jessica *always* insisted on having her own way. Once at a shopping center, she refused to accompany her parents back to their car. Instead, she forced them to chase her through parked cars and traffic. Severe scoldings and spankings were completely ineffective in stopping her "brat" behavior. Jessica was in charge!

Early in my experience as a psychologist, I worked with Jessica and Mrs. Stiles, her mother. Mrs. Stiles agreed to try counseling although she was pessimistic about changing her daughter. I didn't do therapy with Jessica. Instead, I taught Mrs. Stiles effective methods of discipline and child management. She correctly applied these methods and after a stormy eight weeks, *Jessica's behavior changed dramatically!* She didn't become an angel, but she became manageable.

During our counseling sessions, Mrs. Stiles was always a little upset with me. She was annoyed because I gave professional advice in managing Jessica when I had no children of my own. Also, she felt that I hadn't fully appreciated how difficult it was being Jessica's mother.

Several months after we concluded parent counseling, Mrs. Stiles learned that my wife was expecting our first child. What was Mrs. Stiles' reaction upon hearing the good news? She exclaimed, *"I hope that Dr. Clark's kid is as mean as a snake! Then he'll know what I had to put up with!"*

Although you may not have a "Jessica," chances are that you do have a child who isn't always an angel. *SOS! Help For Parents* can help you to become a more self-confident and effective parent. You'll learn many new methods for improving your child's behavior. As a result, your child will be better behaved and happier. Your life will be simpler and more pleasant.

This book is your guide for handling a variety of common behavior problems. We'll look at specific solutions to problems such as the following:

Problems Parents Face

- Your three-year-old hits you when he doesn't get his way. You have tried scolding and spanking but his behavior is getting worse.

- It embarrasses and angers you when your ten-year-old daughter talks back to you whenever you ask her to do a simple chore. When you explain to her how impolite her "back-talk" is, she mocks you.

- You dread Saturday mornings. Your twelve-year-old and eight-year-old regularly engage in Saturday morning arguing and fighting while watching television. You repeatedly *warn* them to stop arguing and fighting. But really you have nothing effective to back up your warnings.

- Your five-year-old daughter has started having tantrums. She is even having tantrums in the homes of your friends. You are tired of her behavior and tired of making excuses for her. You feel helpless to change her.

The behavioral approach to child rearing and discipline is very useful in understanding children and helping them to change. What is the behavioral approach? What is behavioral discipline? *The behavioral approach states that good and bad behavior are both learned.* It also maintains that behavior can be "unlearned" or changed. *Behavioral discipline* offers specific methods, skills, procedures, and strategies for parents to use in getting improved behavior from their children.

You can be optimistic about helping your child to change! Behavioral methods are extremely effective in changing all kinds of problem behaviors. Child research studies show a 50 to 90 percent reduction in a wide variety of problem behaviors with the use of behavioral methods.[26,41,69] Research demonstrates the effectiveness of these methods for children in the United States and in various foreign countries including West Germany,[34,35] Japan,[54] Britain,[47,72] Canada,[5,74] Mexico,[45,65,70] The Netherlands,[22] Belgium,[43] and in Scandanavian countries.[53] As a parent and psychologist, I have considerable confidence in these methods. In fact, I have used nearly all the behavioral methods described in this book with my own children. These skills are easy to learn, and they work!

"No one told us that it would be like this!"

How To Use This Book

Read Chapters 1 through 12 before you actually begin using these new strategies with your child. Understanding the methods, step-by-step instructions, and examples in these chapters will enable you to be successful in guiding your child to improved behavior. Also, you will learn to avoid common pitfalls and mistakes when managing your child.

At the end of each chapter is a section called "Main Points To Remember." These are the most important ideas and instructions contained in each chapter.

Small numbers are listed throughout the book. These numbers refer to sources of information or references which are listed at the end of the book.

SOS! Help For Parents is based on my professional practice as a psychologist, my personal experience as a parent, and the results of numerous parent-child research studies. Managing one's children is a challenging and sometimes humbling task, even for psychologists and family counselors. My wife (an elementary teacher) and I use the methods of discipline and child management described in this book with our two sons. We began using these methods when they were toddlers.

More than fifteen years after working with Mrs. Stiles and Jessica, I still think about Mrs. Stiles and her "good wishes" for my firstborn! I have continued to study child management, not only to help parents, but because I certainly didn't want to be cursed with *"a kid as mean as a snake"*!

Chapter 1

Why Kids Behave And Misbehave

UNCOOPERATIVE BEHAVIOR   COOPERATIVE BEHAVIOR

"No! . . . I won't do it!"   *"Whew! . . . This is hard work."*

Why do some children sail through childhood with few noticeable behavior problems, whereas others are a constant problem to their parents? Children, as well as adults, find these "problem kids" obnoxious and either complain about them or avoid them. It's as though some problem kids lie awake at night plotting their next day's misbehavior.

As a psychologist, I've had a firsthand look at the feelings of frustration and failure which many parents experience. Frustrated parents *are* lying awake at night, desperate for some solutions.

Solutions do exist! With increased knowledge of the rules and methods for improving behavior, parents can help their children to be better behaved and more agreeable family members.

Both good and bad behavior are shaped by the rewards which the child receives. Sometimes parents "accidentally" reward and strengthen their child's bad behavior. Three-year-old Patrick may get to stay up well past his bedtime (a reward) if he "wears his parents down" with relentless complaining and crying. Your child's bad behavior will grow stronger if you or other people reward it. Behavior which is *not* rewarded or *is* punished, will grow weaker and be less likely to occur in the future.

There are three basic child rearing rules which parents should follow. The rules *look* simple! You can easily see what all of your friends are doing wrong with *their* children. However, when you try to use these rules with *your* child you can appreciate how difficult it is to be consistent and effective. Remember these rules!

Three Child Rearing Rules—

Parents' Check List

Rule #1. Reward good behavior (and do it quickly and often).*

Rule #2. Don't "accidentally" reward bad behavior.**

Rule #3. Punish some bad behavior (but use *mild* punishment only).

RULE #1   Reward Good Behavior (And Do It Quickly And Often)

Children learn to talk, dress themselves, share toys, and do chores because they receive attention and other types of rewards from their parents and other people. As parents, we should frequently and abundantly reward the good behavior of our children.

An adult holds a job and in return receives a paycheck and recognition from others. A paycheck and recognition are powerful rewards for working. Most of us would stop working if we weren't rewarded for our effort. Rewards shape and determine the behavior of adults and children.[73] Rewards are also called reinforcers.

When a child gets a reward for engaging in a particular behavior, that behavior is strengthened or reinforced. This means that the behavior is more likely to occur in the future. People repeat behavior when they are rewarded. We continue going to work because we get paid. If your child behaves in a way which pleases you, be sure

---

*When behavior is rewarded, that behavior receives "positive reinforcement" or simply "reinforcement."

**When behavior which once was rewarded is no longer rewarded, the term "extinction" is used. Extinction is also called nonreinforcement of behavior.

to strengthen that behavior by frequently rewarding it. What type of rewards should you use? Read on!

Social rewards are very effective in strengthening the desirable behavior of both children and adults. Social rewards include smiles, hugs, pats, kisses, words of praise, eye contact, and attention. A hug or a kind word is easy to give. That's good because children need lots of social rewards to strengthen their appropriate behavior.

Hugs are powerful *social rewards* for children
—and for parents as well.

Some parents are stingy with their praise and attention. They may say that they are too busy or that their child ought to demonstrate good behavior without being rewarded for it. Parents who are stingy with smiles, hugs, and words of praise don't realize the powerful affect of frequently rewarding their child's desirable behavior. If four-year-old Emily straightens her room or helps you with chores, you need to tell her that you appreciate it. If you don't, she will be less likely to help with chores in the future.

Praise is more effective in strengthening your child's desirable behavior if you praise the specific behavior rather than your child. After your daughter cleans and straightens her room, praise her behavior by saying, *"Your room looks great and you did such a good job cleaning it!"* That statement of praise is more effective than saying, *"You are a good girl."* Develop the habit of praising the specific behavior or actions which you want strengthened.

Besides social rewards, there are also *material rewards and activity rewards* such as a special dessert, a small toy, nickels and dimes, a trip to the Dairy Queen, or getting to help mother bake a cake. For most children, however, social rewards are much more powerful than material rewards. In addition, social rewards are more convenient for parents to use. You are the main source of rewards for your child.

Rewards Children Like

Social Rewards	Activity Rewards Including Privileges	Material Rewards
Smiles	Play cards with mother	Ice cream
Hugs	Go to park	Ball
Pats	Look at book with father	Money
Attention	Help bake cookies	Book
Touching	Watch a late TV movie	Jump rope
Clap hands	Have a friend over	Balloons
Winks	Play ball with father	Yo-yo
Praise	Play a game together	Flashlight
"Good job"	Go out for pizza together	Special dessert
"Well done"		Record

To be effective, rewards must *immediately* follow the child's desirable behavior. If your daughter takes out the trash (even if that is her regular chore), you should thank her immediately after the task is done—not an hour or so later. All of us like to receive rewards for good behavior as immediately as possible. Children often ask to receive material rewards *before rather than after* they do a chore or engage in a desirable behavior. If you sometimes use material rewards, be sure you give them only *after* the desirable behavior occurs.

RULE #2 Don't "Accidentally" Reward Bad Behavior

When a child's misbehavior is accidentally rewarded, that misbehavior is strengthened and is more likely to occur again in the future. Often, busy or preoccupied parents unintentionally reward their child for engaging in behavior which is undesirable or inappropriate. *When parents reward bad behavior, they are causing future problems for themselves as well as for their children.* This is probably one of the most common child rearing mistakes which parents make.

"ACCIDENTALLY" REWARDING BAD BEHAVIOR

JOHN ROBB

"But, I don't want to go to bed! I'm not tired. . . ."

"Calm down! You can stay up another 30 minutes. I can't stand to hear you cry and carry on. . . ."

Your child may have learned that he can delay going to bed at night by complaining, crying, and becoming "emotionally upset" when you say it's bedtime. After his complaining and crying have become intolerable, have you ever "given in" and let him stay up longer? If you have given in, then you have unintentionally rewarded him for crying and becoming emotionally upset. Complaining, crying, and getting upset are behaviors which then are more likely to occur in the future. These behaviors are learned and reinforced just like appropriate and desirable behaviors are learned and reinforced. Don't reward bad behavior or behavior which you don't want.

Teaching Nathan To Whine

When five-year-old Nathan wants his mother's attention, especially when she is busy, he begins to whine. Mother finds his whining so unbearable that she stops whatever she is doing, scolds him for whining, and then asks what is troubling him. Nathan has learned that when he *really* wants his mother's attention, he first must whine and accept a mild scolding. Then he gets his mother's attention—a powerful reward for five-year-old Nathan. Mother has taught Nathan to whine.

Also, *children teach parents to behave in certain ways.* Nathan has taught his mother to give him attention when he whines. When she gives him attention, he rewards *her* by stopping his whining. *Children and parents "teach" each other both appropriate and inappropriate behaviors.*[56]

THE STRONG-WILLED CHILD

"I'm ready to eat NOW!"

The strong-willed child can become skillful and powerful in controlling her parents, siblings, and peers. She uses "control-by-pain."[58]

The strong-willed child is another example of how parents and others can accidentally reward bad behavior and cause that behavior to become a severe problem. Watching a child cry and have a temper tantrum is distressing and emotionally upsetting for most people. To stop her persistent crying and tantrum behavior, parents and other people eventually give in to her demands. Thus, the strong-willed child learns to force others to give in to her demands by causing them emotional pain and discomfort.

A strong-willed child may achieve considerable power and

control over her parents and others. To get her way, she may engage in endless pestering and complaining, yelling and crying, or physical attacks on her parents, siblings, and peers. Only when others give her what she wants will she stop causing them stress and emotional pain.[58] With boundless energy and endurance, she forces her parents and others to reward her bad behavior. However, parents can help the strong-willed child by using the methods and skills outlined in this book.

RULE #3 Punish Some Bad Behavior
(But Use *Mild* Punishment Only)

Parents need to use *mild* punishment in order to decrease or eliminate some unacceptable or dangerous behavior.

Christy Loses Her Tricycle

Mother saw four-year-old Christy ride her new tricycle into the street. That was against the rule and the rule already had been explained to Christy.

Immediately, Mother walked out to the street, removed Christy from her tricycle, and harshly scolded her. Mother also said, *"Christy, for riding in the street — you can't ride your tricycle for a week."* The tricycle was put away. It was seven days before Christy could play with it again.

Parents dislike punishing their children. They prefer to reward good behavior. However, the correct use of *mild* punishment is often essential in helping a child. You'll learn about the use of *mild* punishment such as scolding, natural consequences, logical consequences, time-out, and behavior penalty. However, don't use *severe* punishment, such as grim threats or hard spankings. This often complicates problems.

Errors To Avoid In Child Rearing: A Summary

Do follow the basic child rearing rules discussed previously. Also, avoid making the following four errors. These parenting errors can contribute to behavior problems or emotional problems in children.

Examples Of Child Rearing *Errors*

Error #1
Parents Fail To Reward Good Behavior

Example—Brian, a fourth grader, walks up to his father carrying his report card. Father, in his easy chair, is busy reading the newspaper. Father fails to reward his son for getting good grades in school.

Brian: *"I made pretty good grades this term. Would you like to see my report card, Dad?"*

Father   *"Yes, but let me finish reading the paper first . . . Would you go and ask Mother if she paid the bills today?"*

"Accidentally" Causing Behavior Problems— Four Child Rearing *Errors To Avoid*

Error #1. Parents fail to reward good behavior.

Error #2. Parents "accidentally" punish good behavior.

Error #3. Parents "accidentally" reward bad behavior.

Error #4. Parents fail to punish bad behavior (when *mild* punishment is indicated).

Error #2
Parents "Accidentally" Punish Good Behavior

Example—Eight-year-old Sarah wants to surprise Mother by washing the lunch dishes. Mother unintentionally says something punishing.

Sarah: *"I washed the dishes, Mother. Are you glad?"*

Mother: *"It's about time you did something to help around here. Now, what about the pans on the stove? Did you forget about them? . . ."*

Error #3
Parents "Accidentally" Reward Bad Behavior

Example—Six-year-old Stephanie and her parents are camping and have just arrived back at camp with groceries for lunch. Mother is hot, tired, and hungry.

Stephanie: *"I want to go swimming before lunch."*

Mother: *"First we eat lunch and have a nap, then you can go swimming."*

Stephanie: *"I'll cry if I can't go swimming!"*

Mother: *"Oh Stephanie, anything but that! Go ahead and swim first."*

Error #4
Parents Fail To Punish Bad Behavior
(When *Mild* Punishment Is Indicated)

Example—Mother and Father are sitting in the family room. Both observe eleven-year-old Mark impulsively hit his younger brother on the ear. Neither parent scolds Mark or uses any other form of mild punishment for his aggressive behavior.

Mother: *"I wish you would handle your son."*

Father: *"Boys will be boys!"*

Physical Problems May Contribute To Behavior Problems

Being hungry or overly tired can temporarily lower your child's capacity for self-control and intensify his bad behavior. Certain medical conditions can also increase the likelihood of behavior problems. If you suspect that your child has a medical condition, take him to your family physician or pediatrician for a checkup.

Even though a chronic physical condition may contribute to his bad behavior, keep working on improving his behavior. All the rules and methods discussed in this book are entirely suitable for helping children with handicaps or other physical problems. Succeeding chapters will show you *when and how* to use effective methods for helping your child to improve his behavior.

Main Points To Remember:
1. Both good and bad behavior are strengthened when rewarded.
2. Reward your child's good behavior quickly and often.
3. Avoid rewarding your child's bad behavior.
4. Use *mild* punishment to decrease or eliminate some bad behaviors.

Chapter 2

Clear Communication Promotes Effective Parenting

PROBLEMS FAMILIES FACE—*POOR COMMUNICATION*

JOHN ROBB

Mother and father must maintain clear communication between themselves and agree on goals.

Parents must agree about which behaviors are desirable and undesirable for their child. Otherwise, their son or daughter may become confused about what is expected of them and behave badly as a result.

Clear and frequent communication between spouses promotes effective parenting. Likewise, clear communication between you and your child is also essential for helping him to improve his behavior. Good communication requires a lot of talking and listening by all family members. Your child needs clear communication, discipline, and love from you.

Parents Must Agree On Goals

You and your spouse must determine which of your child's behaviors are good or desirable and which are bad or undesirable. Your basic values determine the goals and standards of behavior which you set for your child. Reward and strengthen your child's good behavior and eliminate or weaken unacceptable behavior by failing to reward it.

PARENTS SOLVING PROBLEMS

Clear communication between mother and father is important.

Both Rewarding *And* Punishing David's Baby Talk

When four-year-old David wanted something or just wanted attention, he often used "baby talk." If he was thirsty, he would point to the kitchen faucet and say, *"wa-wa"*. David's mother thought his baby talk was cute and often rewarded it (getting him a drink of water when he said, *"wa-wa"*). David's father thought his baby talk was obnoxious, scolded him for it, and called him a "sissy."

David was being rewarded *and* punished for using baby talk. As the days passed, David became more and more emotional, cried easily, and began avoiding his father.

Rewarding and punishing a child for the same behavior is unfair and may cause emotional or behavior problems. Both parents need to decide which behaviors are desirable and which are undesirable.

If you are "single-parenting" your child, clarify your goals and set realistic expectations for your child's behavior by frequently talking with another adult who also cares for your child. Grandparents or a babysitter may be helping to rear your child on a day-to-day basis. If so, be sure that you and the other adult have consistent expectations and goals for your child.

Clear Communication Between Parent And Child

Both you and your spouse need to jointly determine the rules which you want your child to follow. When possible, encourage your child to participate when making rules or modifying them. If he helps to set a rule, he is more likely to follow it and less likely to resent it. Once a rule is decided, however, you should expect him to follow it. He needs to know which of his behaviors you like and which ones are unacceptable. Of course, never tell him that he is a "bad child." However, do tell him which *behaviors* you consider bad or intolerable.

The Twins Help To Set A Rule

Gregory and Adam, four-year-old twins, loved to "roughhouse" and wrestle with each other in the house. Wrestling in the house was okay when they were two years old and when they were very small. However, they were growing rapidly and the house was taking a beating.

Mother and Father sat down with them and explained that they were "bigger now" and that a new rule was needed. The twins asked, *"Can we wrestle in the family room if we don't do it anyplace else?"* Their parents agreed and a new rule was born: *"No wrestling anyplace in the house—except in the family room."*

Whenever you establish a rule, your children should know the rule well enough to repeat it when asked to do so. The parents of Gregory and Adam helped their twins to learn the rule by saying it with them. Mother or Father could ask, *"What is the rule about wrestling?"* and either Gregory or Adam would respond, *"The rule is—no wrestling anyplace in the house, except in the family room."*

How To Give Effective Commands

"Please pick up your toys," is a simple request. *"Stop throwing food!"* or *"Come here and hang up the coat that you threw on the floor!"* are commands.

Parents of children who don't mind are often unable to give clear, emphatic directives or commands to their children.[27] All parents, especially parents of hard-to-handle children, must be able to give clear, effective instructions or commands, on occasion. A parent who uses time-out, an effective method of discipline, must be able to tell his child, *"Go to time-out immediately!"* Learning to give commands doesn't mean that you should start barking commands like an army drill sergeant or that your ten-year-old is about to enter basic training. However, if your child usually doesn't mind and even sasses you when you scold him for not minding, you must be able to give clear, effective commands and to "back up" your commands.

When are commands given? Give your child a command when you want him to *stop* a specific misbehavior *and* you believe that he might disobey a simple request to stop the misbehavior. Also, give a command when you want your child to *start* a particular behavior *and* you believe that your child might disobey a simple request to start the behavior.

How should you give a command? Assume that you come into the living room and find Jennifer, your "hard-to-handle" seven-year-old, jumping up and down on your new sofa. You should walk right up to her, have a stern facial expression, look her in the eye, and maintain eye contact. Call her name and then give her a clear, direct command in a firm tone of voice. Say, *"Jennifer, jumping on the furniture is against the rule. Get off the sofa!"* You have given her a clear command.

Give clear, explicit commands rather than vague ones. Your child is more likely to mind if you say, *"Come here and start putting those toys on the shelf!"* He is less likely to comply with a vague statement such as, *"Do something with all those toys!"*

Don't ask a question or make an indirect comment when you give a command such as, *"It's not nice to jump on the sofa."* Don't say to Jennifer, *"Why are you jumping on the sofa?"* She just might smile at you and say, *"Because it's lots of fun!"*

Also, *don't give your reasons for a rule while the bad behavior is taking place.* The time to explain a rule is before your child breaks it or after the bad behavior stops. Do *not* say to Jennifer while she is still bouncing up and down, *"You shouldn't be jumping on the sofa. It cost a lot of money. We still owe the finance company on it. The springs might come loose. . . ."* However, do say to Jennifer, *"Get off the sofa!"*

After you give your command, Jennifer will probably decide to mind you and get off the sofa. However, let's assume that Jennifer decides to *disobey* your command. She may decide to test you and see if you have anything with which to "back up" your command. It's not necessary to severely punish or threaten to punish Jennifer in order to back up your command. This might further complicate an already difficult parent-child problem.

You have a very simple and effective backup for your command. You have *"time-out!"* Later, in Section Two, we'll discuss how to use time-out in such a confrontation—and without your getting intensely angry. For now, remember the following simple steps for giving effective commands. Memorize and, if necessary, practice these steps.

Giving Effective Commands To Your Child[27,24]
Parents' Check List

✔___ Steps To Follow:

___ 1. Move close to your child.

___ 2. Have a stern facial expression.

___ 3. Say his or her name.

___ 4. Get and *maintain* eye contact.

___ 5. Use a firm tone of voice.

___ 6. Give a direct, simple, and clear command.

___ 7. "Back up" your command, if necessary.

A WELL-ADJUSTED CHILD

A child who is personally and socially well-adjusted feels good about himself *and* about others. He feels *"I'M OK"* and he feels *"YOU'RE OK."* [39]

A well-adjusted child is both loved and disciplined by his parents. He respects the rights of others and he presses others to respect his rights.

Children Need Discipline And Love

Discipline means teaching a child self-control and improved behavior. Your child learns self-respect and self-control by receiving both love and discipline from you. We discipline our children because we love them and we want them to become responsible, competent adults. Being an effective parent requires love, knowledge, effort, and time. This book will teach you basic principles of behavior *and* practical skills for helping your child. To actually help your child, however, you must *practice* these skills and you must provide effort and time, as well as love.

"Reasons" Parents Don't Discipline Their Kids

There are various reasons why some parents avoid disciplining their children. These parents need to be aware of why they are hesitating to discipline and to overcome their resistance to disciplining. You can't expect your child to change her behavior if you are not first willing to change your own behavior. The following are various reasons why parents sometimes find it difficult to change their own behavior.

- **The Hopeless Parent.** This parent feels that her child is unable to change and will always behave badly. She has given up on her child.

"In And Out Of The Garbage Can"

It was the end of the school day and Mrs. Williams had stopped to talk about her son, Kevin, with his first grade teacher. Whenever possible, Mrs. Williams complained about her son's bad behavior to whoever would listen. However, she never attempted to actually discipline her young son.

While Mrs. Williams and Kevin's teacher were talking, Kevin was down the hall playing near a large open garbage can. Mrs. Williams said, *"I can't do a thing with Kevin. He never does what he is supposed to do."*

As mother and teacher talked, and as they continued to watch Kevin from a distance, Kevin crawled in and out of the large garbage can!

Kevin's teacher said, *"Do you see what Kevin is doing? He is going in and out of that garbage can!"* Mother responded with *"Yes, he is always doing something like that. Only yesterday, he jumped in a mud puddle and. . . ."*

Never once did Mother give Kevin a command such as *"Get out of the garbage can!"* She *never* asked him to stop what he was doing. She never actively helped Kevin to improve his bad behavior. Mother had given up on her young son.

- **The Nonconfronting Parent.** This parent avoids confronting his child. He really doesn't expect his child to mind and his child realizes this. Sometimes this parent fears he will lose his child's love if he makes any demands on him. Hearing "I hate you," "You're a terrible father," or "I wish I had a new Daddy" completely devastates this parent and neutralizes his will to discipline.

- **The Low Energy Parent.** He or she can't seem to muster the parenting energy necessary to keep up with an active or misbehaving child. Sometimes, a mother or father is "single-parenting" a child *and* holding a full-time job. Occasionally, the "low energy parent" is suffering from a short-term or chronic depression.

"THE LOW ENERGY PARENT"

"Where did he get all of his energy? He certainly didn't get it from me. I feel tired and worn out all the time—especially when I watch him. . . ."

- **The Guilty Parent.** This parent blames herself for her child's problems and feels especially guilty when she attempts to discipline her child. Self-blame and guilt prevent her from teaching her son or daughter improved behavior. She becomes permissive and passive as a parent.

- **The Angry Parent.** Many parents become emotionally upset and angry each time they discipline their child. Since they can't discipline without being angry and upset and feeling miserable as a consequence, they simply ignore their child's misbehavior. The time-out method, however, helps you to be composed when you correct your child.

- **The Hindered Parent.** Sometimes a parent is hindered by a spouse when attempting to discipline their child. If this happens to you, continue talking with your spouse about desirable goals for your child. After agreeing on acceptable *goals,* work on getting agreement on appropriate *methods of discipline.* Sometimes relatives or friends interfere with discipline. Frequently the same people who get upset if you *do* discipline your child, also get upset if you *don't* discipline your child! Don't let others discourage you from being an effective and self-confident parent.

- **The Troubled Parent.** Marital problems and other difficult life situations sometimes become a heavy burden for a parent. Often, this parent lacks sufficient energy, time, and motivation to help his or her child.

Parenting a child and "holding a family together" is a difficult and challenging task. Psychologists and other professionals can help parents to gain increased understanding of themselves and their family and can help them to improve their parenting skills.

Main Points To Remember:
1. Parents must agree about which behaviors are desirable and undesirable.
2. Clear communication must occur between you and your child.
3. You must be able to give clear and effective commands.
4. Your child needs your discipline as well as your love. If something is preventing you from disciplining your child, determine what it is and work toward correcting it.

Chapter 3

Ways Of Increasing Good Behavior

"That's great! You're learning to tie your own shoes!"

Encouragement, words of praise, and a loving touch strengthen good behavior.

Do you remember teaching a child how to tie his shoes? You first showed him how to do it. Then you asked him to try. When he attempted this new task, you gave him lots of attention and encouragement. He responded by working even harder to please you.

Your encouragement, close attention, smiles, hugs, pats, and words of approval are extremely important to your child and strengthen his behavior. This chapter will show you various methods of rewarding your child in order to get good behavior from him.

Just as it's important to reward your child's good behavior, it's also important to "fail to reward" bad behavior. When you see behavior which you don't want to continue, be sure that you actively ignore it.

Use Active Ignoring

Active ignoring is briefly removing all attention from your misbehaving child. Active ignoring is being sure that you don't accidentally reward his bad behavior with attention.* This method of managing children is particularly effective in reducing the tantrum behavior of toddlers and preschoolers. If you scold or attend to your child while he is having a tantrum, you might unintentionally reward that behavior. Try active ignoring to weaken his behavior. If your child is in a safe place, walk out of the room and wait until his tantrum ceases before returning. Or, you might turn your back and pretend to be absorbed in something else. When his bad behavior stops, give him lots of attention. Also, be sure that your child's bad behavior doesn't *drive* you into giving him a material reward (such as cookies before dinner) or an activity reward (such as watching a late TV movie on a school night).

ACTIVE IGNORING

"I'll be glad when he stops his temper tantrum. I'm getting bored looking at these flowers. . . ."

Good for mother! She is using active ignoring—withdrawing her attention and herself from her misbehaving child.

---

*Active ignoring of inappropriate behavior enables you to follow Child Rearing Rule #2, "Don't 'accidentally' reward bad behavior," described in Chapter 1. Not rewarding a particular bad behavior is called *"extinction"* and it weakens that bad behavior.

Use *active ignoring* to weaken these misbehaviors:

- Whining and fussing

- Pouting and sulking

- Loud crying intended to "punish" parents

- Loud complaining

- Insistent begging and demanding

- Breath holding and mild tantrums

How do you use active ignoring? Follow the points listed in the table.

Use *Active Ignoring*
For Some Misbehaviors

✓	Guidelines To Follow:
___ 1.	Briefly remove all attention from your child.
___ 2.	Refuse to argue, scold or talk.
___ 3.	Turn your head and avoid eye contact.
___ 4.	Don't show anger in your manner or gestures.
___ 5.	Act absorbed in some other activity—or leave the room.
___ 6.	Be sure your child's bad behavior doesn't get him a material reward.
___ 7.	Give your child lots of attention when his bad behavior stops.

Active ignoring often helps to reduce misbehavior. However, when it doesn't, consider using one of the other methods described in this chapter or in succeeding chapters.

Reward Good Alternative Behavior

If the undesirable "target behavior" is whining, then the alternative behavior is talking in a normal tone of voice. If your daughter normally whines when she wants something, then you should praise her when she asks for something without whining. *Reward the alternative behavior in order to strengthen it.* *

Rewarding Good Alternative Behavior—
Examples For Parents

Target Behavior To Be Decreased (Use active ignoring or mild punishment)	*Good* Behavior To Be Increased (Use praise and attention)
1. Whining	1. Talking in a normal tone of voice
2. Toy Grabbing	2. Toy sharing; toy trading
3. Temper tantrums when frustrated	3. Self-control when frustrated
4. Hostile teasing	4. Playing cooperatively
5. Swearing	5. Talking without swearing
6. Hitting	6. Solving problems using words

Assume that Christopher, your four-year-old, usually has a temper tantrum when he doesn't get what he wants—like when he doesn't get a cookie just before dinner. The next time you turn down one of his requests, be sure to reward him with praise if he demon-

---

*Using rewards to increase good behavior which is alternative to the undesirable target behavior is called "reinforcement of alternative behavior" or "differential reinforcement of other behavior."[75]

strates self control. Say to him, *"Christopher, you didn't get a cookie this time, but you acted grown-up anyway. I'm proud of that grown-up behavior. After we eat dinner you may have three cookies!"*

What behavior has to go? What is the behavior you want? Wait for that good behavior. Then *"catch your child being good"* and reward him. If he doesn't seem to know how to do the desirable behavior, such as toy sharing or toy trading, teach it to him. Teaching the desirable behavior is discussed next.

Help Your Child To Practice Good Behavior

Help your child to practice the behavior that you want her to learn. For example, if your daughter grabs toys away from another child, tell her to "trade toys" instead. Then demonstrate toy trading yourself and help her to actually practice this skill.

Toy-Grabbing Gloria

When three-year-old Gloria wanted a toy from her baby sitter, she often grabbed it. Gloria's parents didn't allow her to keep the toy because that rewarded toy grabbing. However, Gloria persisted.

To help his daughter change, Mr. Scott developed a two-part program. For the first part, Gloria either received a scolding or a time-out when she grabbed a toy.

For the second part, Mr. Scott helped Gloria learn "toy trading." If Gloria wanted a toy truck from her sister, she showed her another toy and then offered to trade toys. Sometimes Gloria offered her baby sister four or five different toys before she finally wanted to trade.

Mr. Scott taught Gloria the skill of toy trading by first demonstrating this skill himself and by having her watch. He traded toys with the baby. Then Gloria practiced toy trading with the baby and Mr. Scott watched. When Gloria was successful, he praised her efforts. However, when Gloria grabbed a toy from her baby sister, he scolded her or placed her in time-out.

Gloria became good at toy trading and also spent more time sharing toys and playing with her sister. Mr. Scott weakened toy grabbing by using a mild punishment. He taught Gloria toy trading to replace toy grabbing.

Use Grandma's Rule

Help your children to do unpleasant tasks by using Grandma's Rule.* *Grandma's Rule states, "After you do your chore, then you get*

---

*Grandma's Rule is also called the Premack Principle.[64]

to play." It's easier to begin and complete an unpleasant task if we get to have fun *afterwards.*

Using Grandma's Rule—
Examples For Parents

After you:	*then* you get to:
1. complete your math homework	1. watch television.
2. wash the supper dishes	2. go out and play ball.
3. straighten your room	3. play video games.
4. take a nap	4. go swimming.
5. eat your vegetables	5. eat dessert.
6. practice the piano for twenty minutes	6. visit a friend.

Don't reverse Grandma's Rule. An example of reversing Grandma's Rule is to say, *"You can watch television now if you promise to do your math homework later tonight."* If your daughter always procrastinates with her math because she hates it, she won't be motivated to finish it *by first watching television.* She will continue avoiding her math. She will also feel guilty or upset for failing to complete it. Promises to begin a task and guilt don't help children to do unpleasant chores. Having fun afterwards is a good motivator.

Getting your child to do something extremely distasteful when *reversing* Grandma's Rule is hard to do—like driving your car somewhere backwards. Use Grandma's Rule correctly.

Set A Good Example

Parents constantly demonstrate or "model" behavior which their children observe. Your child learns how to behave and misbehave by observing and imitating your behavior and the behavior of others.[6] Don't unintentionally demonstrate behavior that you wouldn't like to see in your child.

CHILD REARING *MISTAKES* WHICH PARENTS MAKE

You are an *example* for your child!

Model only behavior that is acceptable for your child
to imitate.

Your child pays particularly close attention to you when you are
frustrated with a problem or having a conflict with another person. *By
watching you, she is learning how she might handle her own frustrations and conflicts with others in the future.*

If you use a lot of sarcasm and criticism in dealing with other
people, you're actually teaching your child to use sassy talk and complaining as a way of dealing with you and other people. By watching
their parents some kids learn that people swear if they get hurt.
Sometimes children even learn to have temper tantrums by watching
their parents lose control of their own emotions and behavior. *You are
a model for your child whether you want to be or not! Be a good model!*

Children also learn by watching people on television and in the
movies. Many programs show people trying to solve interpersonal
problems and conflicts by using aggression and violence. Monitor the
kind of television programs and movies your kids watch.

Be An Organized Parent

Be organized and plan ahead to be an effective parent. Anticipate your child's needs before his bad behavior *forces* you to meet
his needs. When you allow your child's bad behavior to force you to
meet his needs, you unintentionally reward that bad behavior.

If you are shopping with your children, return home before they
are completely exhausted. The time to have a long telephone conversation is not just before supper when your children are hungry and

fussing with each other. If you and your child are spending the evening visiting friends, avoid staying hours past your child's normal bedtime.

Your children, especially if they are young, need a lot of care and supervision. As parents, we really don't go "off duty" until our children are asleep and even then we are "on call." A favorite time of the day for busy mothers and fathers is "after the children are asleep."

HOUSEHOLD CONFUSION

"Listen, Julie, I'm going to have to get off the phone. The kids are starting to get wild!"

Sometimes the entire family situation becomes disorganized. Often, in such a situation, the *misbehavior* of children rapidly intensifies. Reorganize the situation as quickly as you can. Being an effective parent takes not only love and discipline, but a lot of time and planning.

Main Points To Remember:
1. *Encourage and praise* your child's good behavior.
2. *Actively ignore* some misbehaviors.
3. After targeting an undesirable behavior, *reward the good alternative behavior.*
4. Help your child to *practice behavior* that you want him to learn.
5. Use *Grandma's Rule* to help your child perform unpleasant chores.
6. *Set a good example* for your child.

Chapter 4

What Is Time-Out?
When Do Parents Use It?

A "typical tantrum"

Time-out is especially effective for managing impulsive, hard-to-handle behaviors such as tantrums.

Questions Parents Ask

- *"What is time-out?"*

- *"How early can I start using time-out with my toddler?"*

- *"Which of my child's bad behaviors can be decreased by the time-out method?"*

- *"Do other methods of child management work better in certain situations? If so, what are they?"*

31

Time-Out Before Supper

Mary had a long day at the office, picked up four-year-old Jason from day-care, and now was starting supper. Both Mary and Jason were tired and hungry. *"I want that box of cookies,"* Jason demanded, as he pointed to the open cupboard. Mary replied, *"You may have a glass of milk and two crackers to hold you over. Dinner will be ready in 30 minutes. You may have cookies for dessert. . . ."*

She set milk and crackers in front of Jason. He immediately replied, *"I don't want any dumb milk"* and backhanded the glass of milk, sending it across the table and onto the floor. Resisting the urge to "backhand" Jason, she said sternly, *"Time-out! You knocked the glass over. Go now!"* Angry and crying, Jason got down from the table and walked slowly to the time-out place, a utility room at the end of the hall. Mary picked up the small kitchen timer, set it for four minutes, and placed it near the door of the utility room. She then returned to the kitchen.

After four minutes the timer rang. Jason appeared in the kitchen, picked up the two crackers on the table, and turned on the kitchen TV. Looking up at his mother a few minutes later, he said, *"Guess what, Mom, the Roberts got a new puppy. . . ."*

Following Mary's use of time-out, the mother-son relationship quickly returned to normal. Mary kept her "cool" and also quickly dealt with the demanding tantrum behavior of her son.

JASON

"I don't want any dumb milk!"

What Is Time-Out?

In basketball and football, "time-out" is a brief interruption or suspension of play for participants. As a method of discipline, "time-out" is a brief interruption of activities for your child.

Time-out means time-out from reinforcement, rewards, and attention. You quickly remove your child from the reinforcing or pleasurable situation in which his misbehavior occurs and briefly place him in a quiet and boring area which is not reinforcing or enjoyable at all. By placing your child in time-out, you prevent him from getting attention or other rewards following his undesirable behavior.*

Advantages Of Using The Time-Out Method

- Time-out quickly weakens many bad behaviors.

- Time-out helps stop various misbehaviors permanently. Improved behaviors then take their place.

- It's easy for parents to learn and use.

- Parents report feeling less angry and upset when using this method of discipline.

- Parents are a rational and nonaggressive "model" for their kids.

- The parent-child relationship quickly returns to normal following the use of time-out.

The time-out method of discipline has two goals, an immediate one and a long-term one. The immediate goal is to bring an abrupt stop to the problem behavior. The long-term goal of time-out is to help your child to achieve self-discipline.

Time-Out From Your Child's Point Of View

Children don't like time-out because they experience a number of immediate losses even though these losses are brief. When placed in time-out, kids lose attention from their family. They lose power and control and the ability to anger and upset their parents. Kids lose

---

*Time-out is a method of nonreinforcement for undesirable behavior as well as a mild punishment. Time-out is an effective method for following Child Rearing Rule #2, "Don't accidentally reward bad behavior" and Rule #3, "Punish some bad behavior," described in Chapter 1.

the freedom to play with toys and games and to join interesting activities. Since the time-out method is swift and definite, kids are less able to avoid this form of discipline. Children are usually irritated at their parent *when* sent to time-out and *during* time-out. Ordinarily, the child's annoyance rapidly disappears *after* time-out is over.

Sammie

"I'd Rather Get A Spanking!"

Mr. Gordon used the time-out method for several months and was successful in reducing hitting and pushing by his five-year-old son, Sammie. Mr. Gordon greatly decreased his use of swats, spankings, and intense scoldings. He was interested in his son's feelings regarding time-out vs. more aggressive forms of discipline.

On a quiet Saturday afternoon, Mr. Gordon casually asked, *"Sammy, when you hit your little brother, what should Dad do? Spank you or put you in time-out?"* Sammie replied, *"I'd rather get a spanking! I want to get it over with. There is nothing to do in time-out. I don't like time-out!"*

The time-out method is effective in correcting bad behavior because kids hate being in time-out. Many children prefer to get a spanking or a severe scolding rather than briefly being placed in time-out.

Both children and adults resist changing their behavior. Kids don't want to stop their troublesome behaviors. However, if they continue with these problem behaviors, they receive repeated time-outs. Consequently, they find these problem behaviors easier to give up! Kids then explore different ways to meet their needs. When these new behaviors are rewarded, they are strengthened and more likely to occur in the future. Time-out weakens old problem behaviors and encourages new acceptable behaviors to emerge.

Your Child Between Two And Twelve

Parents successfully use the time-out method with children between two and twelve.[14,36,56] However, when you *begin* using time-out with your child, he shouldn't be older than eleven. For the older child, use other methods of child management discussed in this book.

Observe The Bad Behavior Yourself

Ideally, you should *see or hear* the bad behavior so that you may immediately send your child to time-out. To be most effective, place your child in time-out within 10 seconds after the bad behavior. Immediacy of time-out is especially important if your child is between two and four years old.

Bad behavior repeats itself! If you just missed an opportunity to time-out a bad behavior, be patient. Another misbehavior is likely to occur very soon!

Which Misbehaviors Deserve Time-Out?

Time-out is effective in helping to correct persistent misbehaviors which are impulsive, aggressive, emotional or hostile. When time-out is compared with other methods of discipline, *it is one of the most effective methods available for eliminating severe problem behaviors.* Recognize that time-out is not the only method of discipline which can reduce the following misbehaviors.

Category A Behaviors—
Misbehavior Which Deserves Time-Out

Hitting
Temper tantrums
Hostile teasing of other children; provoking others
Sassy talk or back-talk to parents and other adults
Angry screaming and screeching
Toy grabbing from another child
Toy throwing

Misbehavior Which Deserves Time-Out
(Continued)

Destroying toys
Kicking others
Biting or threatening to bite
Hair pulling
Choking others
Spitting or threatening to spit at others
Throwing dirt, rocks or sticks at others
Mistreating or hurting pets and other animals
Obnoxious loud crying "intended" to punish parents
Slapping
Pinching
Scratching
Tattling
Doing dangerous things such as riding a tricycle into the
   street
Whining loudly
Hitting others with an object
Threatening by word or gesture to hit or hurt others
Cursing and swearing
Pushing others standing on a stairway
Food throwing at the dinner table
Purposefully damaging furniture or the house
Mocking or trying to humiliate parents
Loud complaining or demanding behavior, after a warning
Name calling and "making faces" at others
Persistently interrupting adult conversation, after a
   warning
Disobeying a "command" to immediately *stop* a particular
   misbehavior

In looking over this "shopping list" of bad behavior, do you recognize any of your child's behavior which you wish to eliminate? Parents who have used the time-out method have been able to reduce or eliminate each misbehavior in Category A. Whether or not you consider a behavior "bad" or "bad enough" to deserve time-out, depends upon your values and upon the goals which you and your spouse have for your child.

However, time-out is not the solution for all problem behavior of children. Time-out should *not* be used for Category B behavior problems.

Category B Behaviors
Do *Not* Use Time-Out On These Problem Behaviors

Pouting, sulking
Irritableness, bad mood, grumpy
Failing or forgetting to do chores
Failing to pick up clothes and toys
Not doing homework or piano practice
Overactive behavior (but *do* time-out aggressive or
    destructive acts)
Fearfulness
Being dependent, timid or passive
Seclusiveness, wanting to be alone
Behaviors *not* observed by the parent

Use other forms of child management to help with these problem behaviors. Time-out is *not* effective when used on Category B behavior. *Actively ignore* quiet pouting, soft crying, and whimpering (Chapter 3).

Parents often ask if they can use time-out to get their child to *start* doing something which is fairly complex such as, *"Straighten your room"* or, *"Do your homework."* Time-out is effective in *stopping bad behavior.* Threatening your child with time-out doesn't encourage him to *begin* a chore which is both complex and distasteful. To get your child to do a distasteful chore, consider using *Grandma's Rule* (Chapter 5), *token rewards* (Chapter 14), or, for the older child, a *parent-child contract* (Chapter 14).

When you press your child to do a disagreeable chore, she might sass you or have a temper tantrum. Do use time-out on this backtalk or temper tantrum. Once you stop this interfering behavior, it will be easier to get your child to do distasteful chores. Be sure to praise her efforts to begin and complete unpleasant tasks.

Select Only One Or Two "Target" Behaviors

You and your spouse need to select one or two bad behaviors on which to begin the time-out method. These behaviors are called *target behaviors because your aim or goal is to change them.* Use time-out *consistently and repeatedly* on these target behaviors.

Don't *begin* using time-out on all of your child's inappropriate or unacceptable behaviors. He might spend all day in time-out! After gaining success in decreasing the first target behavior, you can select another target behavior to be decreased.

How do you go about selecting a target behavior? Look over the list of Category A misbehaviors and choose one of these or a similar misbehavior. The behavior should be "countable." For example, be able to actually count the number of times that your child sasses you or tattles on a brother or sister.

SELECT A TARGET BEHAVIOR
AND
USE TIME-OUT REPEATEDLY ON THE TARGET BEHAVIOR

"Darn! Busted again! I've got to stop teasing my brother. I land in time-out every time. I'm going to find something else interesting to do besides teasing him. Maybe I'll play my records or visit a friend. . . ."

Time-out is effective because it stops bad behavior (*"teasing my brother"*) and thus allows improved good behavior (*"I'll play my records or visit a friend."*) to emerge. Do use time-out repeatedly to stop the selected target behavior. When the improved good behavior emerges, reward it.

Also, be sure that the target behavior occurs frequently. You won't be able to obtain adequate experience in learning how to use time-out unless the behavior occurs at least once a day.

When first beginning the time-out method you might select two target behaviors, one minor problem behavior and one major problem behavior. Begin using time-out with a minor target behavior such as tattling or teasing. These are easy target behaviors to handle because children are usually not extremely emotional or angry when tattling or teasing.

Later, after getting experience in using time-out, move on to a major target behavior such as hitting or temper tantrums. These misbehaviors are usually more challenging since children are more emotional or angry when demonstrating these behaviors.

Use time-out repeatedly on the target behavior. When first using time-out, use it each time the target behavior occurs. You should see a 50 to 90 percent decrease in the target behavior within one or two weeks.

Count How Often The Target Behavior Occurs

Before you begin using time-out, it's a good idea to actually count and record how often the target behavior occurs. Then, after you have been using time-out for awhile, you can see how much the misbehavior has decreased.

Some parents place tally marks on a wall calendar, a convenient place to keep a record of the target behavior. For example, one mother put a mark on the calendar each time her daughter tattled. Mother didn't bother keeping track of "tattles" all day long—just the tattles which occurred each day from supper-time to bedtime.

A curious thing sometimes occurs if a child sees his parent recording tally marks. Often the child's target behavior abruptly decreases without the parent even using time-out.[44]

You may think it's a nuisance to keep a record of target behavior. However, this record will tell you how effective you have been in reducing your child's misbehavior.

Main Points To Remember:
1. Time-out means *time-out from reinforcement, rewards, and attention.*
2. Select one or two *target behaviors* to be decreased.
3. Use time-out *immediately* after the target behavior occurs.
4. Use time-out *repeatedly* on the target behavior.
5. Follow the *steps for using time-out* which are described in Chapters 6 through 11.

Chapter 5

Major Methods For Stopping Bad Behavior

PROBLEMS PARENTS FACE

How would *you* handle this situation?

Questions Parents Ask About Punishment

- *"Should parents use mild punishment to change misbehavior?"*

- *"What kinds of mild punishment are effective in stopping misbehavior?"*

- *"Can the use of punishment be emotionally harmful to a child?"*

- *"Why do children continue misbehavior for which they are punished?"*

There are five types of mild punishment which parents can use in helping their children. One of these methods, time-out, is brief and is especially effective in stopping persistent misbehavior which is impulsive, emotional, and hard-to-handle.

Other chapters in this book describe, step by step, when and how to use the time-out method. However, time-out does have a limitation. When you use time-out, you should use it *immediately* after the bad behavior occurs. What do you do about serious misbehavior which you discover minutes or hours later?

Four other methods of mild punishment are effective even if you can't apply them immediately. They are: (1) *scolding and disapproval,* (2) *natural consequences,* (3) *logical consequences,* and (4) *behavior penalty.* This chapter will describe how to correctly use these methods.

To be a confident and competent parent, know and use several methods to manage your child's problem behaviors. You can easily learn these effective methods! It's a lot easier to deal with a particular misbehavior if you know several ways to handle it.

Mild punishment can stop or weaken your child's bad behavior. However, it can't increase good behavior when used alone. As emphasized in earlier chapters, you also must frequently *reward good behavior.*

Guidelines For Parents

    ✔—— Points to Remember:

____ 1. Use punishment sparingly.

____ 2. Use mild punishment only.

____ 3. Punish quickly after the bad behavior occurs.

____ 4. Punish when you are in control of yourself.

____ 5. Briefly state a reason for the punishment.

____ 6. Avoid physical punishment.

Punishment is an unpleasant consequence or penalty which follows a behavior. When you use punishment, be sure to observe the correct guidelines.[77]

The correct use of *mild* punishment won't emotionally harm your child. Often it is essential for improving her behavior. However, *severe* punishment can damage her self-concept and can be emotionally harmful to her. Children who are severely punished may become extremely withdrawn or may act more aggressive and belligerent toward others. Mothers and fathers who severely discipline their children frequently carry a heavy burden of guilt.

PROBLEMS PARENTS FACE

"My sister told me to do it. It's not my fault. . . . Let's just forget about punishment this time. . . ."

Being A Rational And Nonaggressive Model

When at their wits' end, parents often try to punish or control their kids by making irrational threats such as, *"You're grounded all summer for doing that!"* or *"I'm going to pull every hair from your head unless you . . .!"* Parents who use severe or frequent spankings as a method of discipline often don't realize that several different methods of *mild* punishment can be more effective in changing behavior.

Children imitate their parents' behavior.[18,33,46] If you shout, make irrational threats, or spank, you are "modeling" this behavior for your daughter to imitate. She may yell, act emotional, or attempt to "manage" others physically. When using time-out discipline, parents are rational and nonaggressive role models for their children.

Your job as a parent is often stressful and upsetting. Sometimes children intentionally try to anger their parents. They enjoy getting attention and controlling their parents by making them angry and emotional. However, you can resist yielding to your anger. You can do it!

You can avoid yelling and screaming, making grim threats, giving harsh spankings, or using other forms of severe or ineffective punishment. Examine the following methods of discipline.

DISCIPLINE *MISTAKES* WHICH PARENTS MAKE

"This will teach you to behave!"   "This will teach you!"

Children imitate the behavior of their parents. By using spankings and threats, you teach your daughter to use aggressive methods to "manage" others.

Using Scolding And Disapproval Correctly[24]

The Missing Cookies

Mother just discovered that seven-year-old Michelle had disobeyed her and eaten most of the chocolate chip cookies being saved for dessert. She walked toward her daughter and in a stern voice said, *"Michelle, I'm very disappointed that you ate the cookies. I was saving them for supper. Now we won't have enough for dessert tonight."*

Michelle's mother is correctly using disapproval, a form of mild punishment commonly used by parents. When you are scolding for bad behavior, move close to your child, look her in the eye, be stern, express your feelings, and name the undesirable behavior. It's important to have self-control and to avoid making sarcastic or belittling remarks.

Be *brief and calm* when scolding your child. Some children enjoy a lengthy tongue-lashing and watching their parent become upset. They like getting the extra attention from their mother or father, even if that attention is negative.

Avoid "nattering" at your child when you want her to improve her behavior. *Nattering is a combination of chattering, nagging, scolding and complaining.*[61] For example, mother might have said to Michelle, *"I'm mad that you ate all the cookies that I was saving for dessert. Another thing, your hair is a mess again and you left all your toys in the living room. You never appreciate what I do for you. Furthermore, . . ."* Nattering doesn't help a child to improve her behavior and it weakens the parent-child relationship. Don't natter at your child!

PROBLEMS PARENTS FACE

Scolding back!

A scolding *doesn't* help some children to improve their behavior. They merely argue or scold back.

Remember to show disapproval of your child's behavior and not of your child. Don't criticize her personality or character. Let her know that you still respect and love her as a person. Instead of saying, *"You are a mean girl for hitting your brother,"* say *"It was mean to hit your brother."* Don't say *"You are a naughty girl."* Do say *"That was a naughty thing to do."* When you scold, be sure to *disapprove of the behavior* and not the child.

An effective time to use disapproval is just as misbehavior is getting started. For example, your two children may begin with playful teasing and then rapidly move on to hostile teasing. When you find this happening, quickly express disapproval. You might say, *"I really don't like the teasing that's going on between the two of you. I don't mind a little teasing, but when it continues, you two frequently get into an argument. I don't want to hear any more teasing this evening!''*

For many children, disapproval is normally sufficient when used alone as a mild punishment. However, if your child usually becomes angry and argues with you when you scold him, then scolding isn't very effective. When scolding and disapproval are *not* effective, consider using time-out or another form of mild punishment.

Signs that scolding and disapproval are *not* effective with your child:

- He usually scolds back, sasses, mocks, or argues with you.

- He ignores you, appears inattentive, or smiles.

- He has a temper tantrum when scolded.

- He seems to enjoy getting the extra attention from you, even though it's negative attention.

Natural Consequences For Bad Behavior[18,20]

PROBLEMS PARENTS FACE

''Let's see. . . . Should I use TIME-OUT or should I let Kitty give NATURAL CONSEQUENCES?''

Allowing *Natural Consequences* To Occur

For Bad Behavior—

Examples For Parents

<u>Bad Behavior</u>	<u>Natural Consequences</u>
1. Handling a cat roughly.	1. Getting scratched.
2. Breaking a toy on purpose.	2. Having a broken toy which is not replaced with a new one.
3. Teasing neighborhood children.	3. Being avoided by neighborhood children.
4. Not doing a homework assignment.	4. Staying after school the next day if required by the teacher.
5. Not wearing gloves on a cold day.	5. Having cold hands.
6. Not combing your hair.	6. Being told by other children that your hair is a mess.
7. Getting ready for school very slowly in the morning.	7. Being late for school and explaining to the teacher why you are late.
8. Pushing and shoving other children of the same age.	8. Getting pushed and shoved back.
9. Carelessly spilling a drink.	9. Not getting a refill.

A natural consequence for not wearing gloves on a cold day is having cold hands. Staying late after school is a natural consequence for not doing a homework assignment.

A natural consequence is an event that normally or naturally happens to a child following his bad behavior, unless his parents step in to prevent the consequence. The parent allows the child to experience the natural consequences of his own behavior unless there is some danger to the child's *safety.*

   If six-year-old James teases a friend, his friend may get angry
and go home. James will be left without a playmate. Being alone is
a natural consequence of teasing one's friend. Consider the various
examples of natural consequences for bad behavior described in the
illustration, "Allowing Natural Consequences To Occur."
   Parents who use natural consequences believe that children
learn to improve their behavior when they are allowed to experience
naturally occurring consequences for their own decisions and actions.
Since punishment is delivered by "nature" and not by parents, children
are much less likely to get angry at their parents for being punished.

Logical Consequences For Bad Behavior[18,20]

Applying *Logical Consequences*

For Bad Behavior—

Examples For Parents

"I'm putting your crayons up for ONE WEEK!"

Bad Behavior	*Logical Consequences*
1. Riding a tricycle into the street.	1. Tricycle is put up for one week.
2. Chewing gum gets stuck to furniture, clothes, or hair.	2. No more gum for five days.
3. Swearing on the telephone.	3. Can't phone out for three days.
4. Mistreating or refusal to care for one's pet.	4. Placing the pet in another home, after several warnings and discussions.
5. Refusal to brush teeth regularly.	5. No more candy or soft drinks until regular tooth brushing is begun.
6. Brother and sister argue and fuss all morning.	6. Family outing to the park is cancelled that afternoon.
7. Not eating the main course at supper.	7. No dessert.

Sometimes parents can't allow natural consequences to occur because it's dangerous to the child. For example, father can't allow three-year-old John to experience *natural* consequences for riding a tricycle into the street. However, father can apply a *logical* consequence—if John doesn't ride his tricycle in a safe place, then he loses the privilege of riding his tricycle for a time. Father can quickly remove the tricycle and not allow John to use it for one week.

When using *logical consequences* to handle problem behavior, *the parent provides punishment for the bad behavior.* Also, the parent makes sure that *the punishment logically fits the nature of the misbehavior. The punishment is a logical or sensible consequence considering the particular bad behavior.* When children see a clear and reasonable relationship between their bad behavior and the punishment, they are more likely to change their behavior. In addition, they are less likely to resent the punishment.

When you apply a logical consequence, it is important to avoid a consequence which is too severe or lasts too long. For example, the consequence of *"No tricycle for two months!"* is too harsh for a three-year-old who rides his tricycle into the street. When angry or emotionally upset by their child's misbehavior, parents frequently declare a consequence which is too extreme. If you make this common mistake, there is a simple solution! Merely tell your child that you made the consequence too severe and that you have reduced the consequence.

The illustration, "Applying *Logical Consequences* For Bad Behavior," gives examples of parents using this method of discipline.

Using Behavior Penalty For Bad Behavior[30]

If you can't think of a logical consequence for a particular misbehavior, then consider using behavior penalty. Behavior penalty is another method of punishment which is effective, but mild. *The child receives some penalty* (such as no television for two days) *following some specific bad behavior* (such as lying to parents).*

The penalty consists of a loss of certain privileges, a fine, or an extra chore which your child finds especially distasteful. *The penalty is not "logically" related to the bad behavior.* For example, each time that nine-year-old Heather mistreats her puppy, she loses the privilege of playing her stereo for the rest of that day. The temporary loss of her stereo (the penalty) is *not* logically related to mistreating her puppy (the behavior). In selecting an effective penalty, Heather's parents

---

*Behavior penalty is also called "response cost" because a child's undesirable response costs her some penalty.

need to know what kind of penalty is most meaningful for Heather. *"No bicycle riding for two days!"* is an ineffective penalty if Heather rarely rides her bicycle anyway.

Using *Behavior Penalty*

For Bad Behavior—

Examples For Parents

"Kids don't like it when I tattle."
"Kids don't like it when I tattle."
"Kids don't like it when I . . . ."

Behavior	*Penalty*
1. Tattling on other children.	1. Child must immediately write three times, *"Kids don't like it when I tattle."*
2. Swearing.	2. A 25 cent fine for each swear word.
3. Lying to parents.	3. No television for two days.
4. Fighting with neighborhood children.	4. No bicycle riding for a week.
5. Refusal to do assigned chores.	5. Cancel plans to spend Friday night with a friend.
6. Persistent teasing of little brother.	6. Stereo and records are "put up" for three days.
7. Failure to clean up one's bedroom by 5:00 p.m.	7. No playing outdoors that evening.

When you use behavior penalty, try to state the penalty *before* the specific bad behavior occurs. For example, Heather's mother might say, *"Heather, your father and I have talked about the way you mistreat your puppy. In the future when you mistreat Scottie, you'll lose the use of your stereo for the rest of the day."* Mother should have Heather *state out loud* the misbehavior and the behavior penalty. This will help her to remember to be kind to Scottie.

The illustration, "Using *Behavior Penalty* For Bad Behavior," gives examples of parents using this method of mild punishment.

In situations where it is not feasible to use natural consequences or logical consequences to handle misbehavior, consider using behavior penalty. Avoid making the penalty too severe or too lengthy, however.

The illustration, "Methods Of Mild Punishment," provides a brief comparison of the five methods of mild punishment discussed in this chapter. These five methods are the most effective forms of mild punishment used by parents. To be successful in handling different types of misbehavior, you should know how to use all five methods.

Time-out is extremely effective, but it should be used only with children between the ages of two and twelve. Also, it should be applied immediately after the bad behavior occurs. Many parents admit that the most difficult behaviors to handle frequently occur right under their noses. Time-out is particularly helpful in stopping these persistent misbehaviors.

The other methods of mild punishment may be used with children who fall within a wide range of ages. These other methods are also *most* effective if applied as quickly as possible after the misbehavior occurs. However, these methods are still rather effective if applied minutes or a few hours after the misbehavior is discovered.

Avoid expressing intense anger when you use punishment. Your child should believe that she got punished because *she* behaved badly and not because *you* got angry.

Bad Behavior Persists Sometimes

Often, children will persist in bad behavior. There are various reasons for this. The amount of reward which the child receives for the bad behavior may far outweigh the punishment. Nichole may tattle on her brother and enjoy getting him into trouble even though mother shows disapproval for her tattling. In this case, Nichole's reward (getting her brother into trouble) outweighs her punishment (receiving disapproval).

Perhaps a child has learned that he runs very little risk of actually being punished. For instance, Aaron may occasionally raid the cookie jar, but rarely get caught. If he is caught, his parents may only threaten to punish, but never follow through with actual punishment.

Sometimes parents demonstrate a particular behavior themselves—such as swearing—for which they punish their child. Children tend to imitate their parents' behavior even if their parents punish them for that behavior.

As a parent, be consistent in the behaviors which you reward and the behaviors which you punish. When you do punish, use punishment which is both mild and effective.

Methods Of Mild Punishment—Comparison For Parents

Method of Mild Punishment	Age of Child	Effectiveness of Punishment	Type of Behaviors Punished	How Quickly Applied
Time-Out	Two through Twelve	Extremely effective	Most behavior, especially hard-to-handle behavior	Immediately, if possible
Scolding and Disapproval	All Ages	Moderately effective	All Behavior	Immediately or later
Natural Consequences	All Ages	Effective	Some Behavior	Immediately or later
"I'm putting your crayons up for ONE WEEK!" Logical Consequences	Three through Adolescence	Effective	Most Behavior	Immediately or later
"Kids don't like it when I tattle." "Kids don't like it when I tattle." "Kids don't like it when I . . . ." Behavior Penalty	Five through Adolescence	Effective	All Behavior	Immediately or later

Main Points To Remember:

1. Rewarding good behavior is the easiest and *best way* to produce desirable behavior.
2. Mild punishment helps stop bad behavior.
3. Use punishment sparingly and use mild punishment only.
4. Be a rational and nonaggressive model when you use punishment.
5. The most effective methods of mild punishment are *time-out, scolding and disapproval, natural consequences, logical consequences, and behavior penalty.*

Section Two

BASIC SKILLS
OF THE TIME-OUT METHOD

Time-out is a powerful method for stopping bad behavior. In this section, you'll learn the basic skills for correctly using time-out. Each "mini-chapter" describes a separate step. If you have questions or problems regarding a particular step when helping your child, you can conveniently review the chapter describing that step. The chapters have separate instructions for managing very young children who are two to four, and for older children who are five to twelve.

Since parents ask many questions about the correct use of time-out, I have used lots of examples and illustrations. The chapters summarize and repeat important points. You'll find these seven mini-chapters particularly easy to read. If you think that your child might not cooperate with the time-out method, refer to Appendix B for solutions.

Let's get started with the time-out method!

Chapter 6

Getting Started With Time-Out

"We have our timer. Let's see what's next. . . ."

Getting started with the time-out method is not difficult.

You can do it! You can help your child to improve his behavior. Using the time-out method, you and your spouse can be more effective and self-confident parents.

This chapter outlines the time-out method and tells you the basic steps to follow in correctly using time-out for the first time. Other chapters of this book will simplify each of these steps.

Immediately place your child in time-out after he demonstrates the undesirable target behavior—such as hitting or sassy talk. Send him there using no more than *10 words and 10 seconds*. He stays one minute in time-out for each year of age.

Remember! *10 words or less, 10 seconds or less in getting there, and one minute in time-out for each year of age.* By using the time-out method, you can be consistent, fair, and effective in helping your child to learn acceptable behavior.

Set a timer for the same number of minutes each time that you place your child in time-out. *Always use a small portable timer.*[24,51,56,60] If you don't have a portable timer now, put one on your shopping list today! The timer keeps accurate track of the time and signals your child when he may leave time-out. *Not using a portable timer is one of the most common mistakes parents make.*

The steps of the time-out method and the number of minutes in time-out are always the same, no matter what your child did. In addition to being effective in changing bad behavior, time-out is easy for parents to use. In fact, unlike other methods of discipline, parents find that time-out gets easier and easier to use.

PROBLEMS PARENTS FACE

"I'm not through coloring yet, DUMB-DUMB!"

Handling sassy talk and back-talk is a common problem parents face.

The example of Cindy shows how one mother began using time-out to greatly reduce her daughter's persistent "sassy talk."

"Time-Out For Sassy Talk"

Cindy was an attractive five-year-old with blue eyes and long blond hair. She was bright, assertive, verbal with adults and children, and generally lovable.

However, Cindy had one bad habit. Cindy was sassy. Cindy was sassy whenever she felt like it. She usually felt like being sassy whenever someone tried to make her do something she didn't want to do. She was sassy with her parents, her grandparents, relatives, and with other children. Even the babysitter complained to Cindy's parents.

Five-year-old Cindy controlled her parents by talking sassy to them. She made them feel helpless and angry. And when others were present, her parents felt embarrassed. When Mr. and Mrs. Miller scolded Cindy for being sassy, she increased her sassy talk. Her behavior was getting worse.

Mr. and Mrs. Miller had heard about the time-out method of discipline and decided to use this method to help their daughter. Sassy talk was the "target" behavior. They were in their fourth day of using time-out, and Cindy already had been placed in time-out eight times.

Cindy's mother was busy cooking and was getting ready to set the table for supper. Cindy was busy coloring on the same table. Carrying a stack of plates, mother said, *"Please pick up your crayons and coloring books so I can set the table."* Cindy ignored her mother's request and continued coloring. Again her mother stated, *"Cindy, pick up your crayons and books, and do it now!"* Cindy responded, *"I'm not through coloring yet, DUMB-DUMB!"* Cindy's mother immediately said, *"Time-out! That was sassy. Time-out in the bathroom."* Pouting, Cindy got down from the table and marched off to the bathroom. Cindy's mother picked up the portable timer, set it for five minutes, and placed it outside the bathroom door.

Five minutes later the timer rang. When Cindy came into the kitchen, Mrs. Miller said, *"Cindy, why did you have to go to time-out?"* Cindy replied, *"I talked sassy to you."* Mother responded, *"Yes, talking sassy put you in time-out."* Mother then continued setting the table.

Good for Cindy's mother! She effectively followed the basic steps of the time-out method. After the target behavior (sassy talk) occurred, she swiftly placed her daughter in time-out, set the timer for five minutes and put it near the time-out place. She didn't spank, scold, or yell at Cindy. Instead, she simply placed Cindy in time-out. As a consequence of her sassy talk, Cindy experienced a number of immediate, but brief losses. She lost the use of her crayons and her mother's attention. She also lost the ability to control her mother by talking sassy to her.

In the coming weeks, and with the repeated use of time-out, Cindy greatly decreased her sassy talk. She found improved ways of talking to her mother and to other adults.

Basic Steps For Using Time-Out

Before you begin the time-out method, be sure to frequently reward your child's good behavior. Also, avoid unintentionally rewarding the behavior on which you plan to use time-out.

In Chapter 4, you learned how to select a target behavior on which to use time-out. Use time-out on this target behavior each time it occurs and not just when you are angry.[56] There should be a major reduction in this target behavior within one or two weeks if you correctly follow the basic steps for using time-out.

Basic Steps For *Initially* Using Time-Out—
Parents' Check List

_____ ✔ Steps To Follow:

_____ 1. Select one target behavior on which to use time-out. (Chapter 4)

_____ *2. Count how often this target behavior occurs. (Chapter 4)

_____ 3. Pick out a boring place for time-out. (Chapter 7)

_____ 4. Explain time-out to your child. (Chapter 8)

_____ 5. Wait patiently for the target behavior to occur. (Chapter 9)

TARGET BEHAVIOR OCCURS!

_____ 6. Place your child in the time-out place and use no more than 10 words and 10 seconds. (Chapter 9)

_____ 7. Get the portable timer, set it to ring in _____ minutes, and place it within hearing distance of your child. (Chapter 10)

_____ 8. Wait for the timer to ring—remove all attention from your child while he waits for the timer to ring. (Chapter 10)

_____ *9. Ask your child, after the timer rings, why he was sent to time-out. (Chapter 11)

*These two steps are important but not essential.

Don't start using time-out, however, until after you have read Chapters 7 through 11. These chapters describe each step of the time-out method and give examples. Also, the instructions in these chapters are tailored for the age of your child.

It's a good idea to look at Chapter 12 and Appendix B before you use time-out for the first time. These sections discuss difficulties which parents occasionally face when first using time-out and how to easily handle these problems.

Main Points To Remember:
1. Send your child to time-out using no more than 10 words and 10 seconds.
2. Time-out lasts one minute for each year of age.
3. Always use a portable timer.
4. Follow the "Basic Steps For Using Time-Out."

Chapter 7

Picking A Boring Place
For Time-Out

"I'll bet my sister is out there having fun. . . ."

The bathroom is a good place for time-out for
children five to twelve years old.

An ideal spot for time-out is a dull place or room where your
child doesn't receive any attention from you or other family members.
Your child should be able to get there quickly, preferably within 10
seconds.

What is the best place in your home for time-out? Look over
the rooms and areas in your home and select a place which is boring
for a child—a place where there is nothing interesting to see or do.

The particular place you select depends on the age of your son
or daughter. *A time-out chair is best for a child between two and four
years old.* A child between five and twelve should be in a separate
time-out room. Since you will use time-out again and again, try a couple of different places and see which one is most effective.

Features of effective time-out places:

- Dull and boring for a child.

- No people; secluded from other family members. (For safety, keep very young children within continual eye sight.)

- Clear of toys, games, television, stereo, books, pets, and interesting objects.

- Safe, well-lighted, and not frightening.

- Can easily get there within 10 seconds.

The Two- To Four-Year-Old

Jimmy And The Time-Out Chair

Three-year-old Jimmy was getting very impatient with his mother. He had been quietly playing with his toy cars for almost fifteen minutes! He wanted his mother's attention, but she was sitting at the kitchen table drinking coffee with a neighbor.

Carrying a big toy truck to his mother he said, *"You have to play with me."* His mother replied, *"Jimmy, when Mrs. Barton and I are finished talking, I will play with you."* *"No, play now!"* Jimmy commanded. He then raised the truck and brought it down on his mother's knee. *"Ouch! Time-out for hitting!"* she responded.

Immediately, she carried Jimmy to a large straight-back chair across the room. Then she set a kitchen timer for three minutes and placed it on the floor several feet from Jimmy's chair. Jimmy began to cry, scream, and "carry on."

She explained to her startled neighbor, *"I've had a lot of trouble with Jimmy hitting me when he doesn't get his way. He used to hit me or try to hit me several times a day. Then I started using a time-out chair for hitting. This is the first time he's hit me in over two weeks. His behavior isn't perfect, but that time-out chair is really helping him to control his hitting."*

If your child is between two and four, an ideal place for time-out is a large, straight-back chair. It's safer than using a separate room for time-out. A large chair is dull and boring, quickly available, and limits your child's activity and movement. In addition, it's difficult for your child to quickly get down from a large chair. Don't use a rocking chair, a small child's chair, the sofa, or an easy chair. These are fun places for toddlers and preschoolers to sit.

You may place the time-out chair in the room with you, in

the adjoining room, or in the hall. For your child's safety, you need to keep an eye on him, but only from the corner of your eye. Don't actually make direct eye contact with your child. You want him to feel that you are ignoring him during his brief time-out. Don't let him catch you looking at him. Some parents avoid giving attention to their child by pretending to read a magazine or newspaper.

JIMMY

"Waah! I won't do it again! I want down! . . ."

A large straight-back chair is a good time-out place for toddlers and preschoolers.

Quickly lift your toddler onto the time-out chair. Next, place the ticking timer several feet from his chair. After the timer rings, lift him down from the chair or tell him that he may get down by himself. In Appendix B, we'll discuss what to do if you think that your child might not stay in time-out.

Let your child sit or kneel on the chair, but not stand or jump or touch his foot to the floor. Some children have tantrums on the chair. Consequently, it shouldn't be placed within kicking or hitting range of the wall or near dangerous or valuable objects.

Parents sometimes place the time-out chair in a corner of the room, turn it to the wall, and make their child face the wall. You may place the chair in a corner. However, *don't* demand that your toddler or preschooler face the wall or corner. Requiring that your child face the wall is overly harsh. Also, it would take constant effort on your part to make him face only one direction. Making him face the wall unintentionally gives him a lot of your attention. Let your child face whatever direction he wants to face. However, do require that he either sit or kneel on the chair.

Your daughter shouldn't take any toys, dolls, or pets to time-out and shouldn't be able to see the television set from her chair. Tell a brother or sister not to pester or talk to her. Warn them that if they do, then they will be sent to a separate chair for time-out!

MISTAKES WHICH PARENTS MAKE WITH TIME-OUT

"Time-out isn't so bad after all! . . ."

How many time-out *mistakes* can you find?

Your child will probably call out to you from her chair, asking for attention and reassurance. She may even say that you are a "bad Mama" or threaten to "run away from home." Actively ignore her and don't answer or make eye contact with her. Answering or looking at her are forms of attention and reduce the effectiveness of time-out. Resist feeling guilty or miserable while she is sitting on the chair. After all, time-out lasts only two to four minutes and will soon be over!

Some parents place their preschooler directly on the floor in the corner of a quiet room or in a semi-deserted hallway rather than using a time-out chair. A particular spot on the floor can be a good place for time-out if your child has learned to stay in one place. However, point to the exact spot where he is supposed to sit.

The Five- To Twelve-Year-Old

Children who are between five and twelve should be placed in a separate room for time-out. It's safer to leave an older child alone in a time-out room than a preschooler who needs close monitoring.

Your home has several good time-out places such as a

bathroom, laundry room, your bedroom, or a deserted utility room or hallway. Usually, the bathroom is the best place for time-out. This might sometimes cause an inconvenience to the rest of the family. Having

A TIME-OUT SPOT ON THE FLOOR

"That timer must be broken. I don't think it's ever going to ring. . . ."

A spot on the floor can be an effective time-out place for very young children.

TIME-OUT IN HIS PARENTS' BEDROOM

"Now why did Dad send me in here? Just because I had a temper tantrum? . . ."

a problem child, however, can cause an even bigger inconvenience to family members! At first, your child might seem to enjoy playing in the water or making paper airplanes out of facial tissue while in the bathroom. However, he will soon get tired of this. While waiting in time-out, a child frequently says that he needs to use the bathroom. Needing to use the bathroom isn't a problem for your child if he is *already* there! *The bathroom is an excellent time-out place.*

Before you first begin using time-out, be sure to prepare the time-out room. *Besides being dull and free of interesting objects, it should also be made safe.* Any objects which might be dangerous, such as glass, sharp objects, medications or poisonous cleaning chemicals, should be removed from the room. After your child settles down and adjusts to time-out, you might return most of the objects to the room. *Place the timer several feet outside the door so that your child can hear it while it is ticking and when it rings.*

Don't Use Your Child's Bedroom

MISTAKES WHICH PARENTS MAKE WITH TIME-OUT

"She actually seems to enjoy time-out in her bedroom! . . ."

Your child's bedroom may seem to be the most "convenient" place for time-out. However, the effectiveness of the time-out method will be severely reduced if you use your child's bedroom. A time-out place should be dull and boring with nothing interesting to do or see. A child's room usually has toys, games, a radio, stereo, or books. It's not dull and boring. Be effective when you use time-out. Resist the temptation to use your child's room as a time-out place.[30,36,56]

After going to the time-out room, your child can do whatever he wants as long as he doesn't make a mess or destroy things. He can sit, stand, or walk around the room. If he makes a mess, like scattering objects around the room or spilling water on the floor, he must clean it up. If he damages something, he must help pay for it. Effective methods for easily handling occasional rebellious time-out behavior are discussed in Appendix B.

Don't Use A Frightening Time-Out Place

MISTAKES WHICH PARENTS MAKE WITH TIME-OUT

"Time-out with Dageon the Dragon! . . ."

"Dageon The Dragon!"

Several years ago I counseled Mr. and Mrs. Meyers regarding ways they could help Bennie, their five-year-old son. Bennie was energetic and difficult to handle. He often grabbed toys away from his little sister or hit her.

We decided to use time-out for hitting and toy grabbing. Mr. and Mrs. Meyers were supposed to discuss this method between themselves but *not* use it until we had another appointment to discuss the correct steps. However, when we met the following week, I was shocked to learn that they had tried to frighten Bennie with time-out.

They told Bennie that if he hit his little sister or grabbed toys away from her, he would have to go to the basement for time-out. They further explained that a dragon named Dageon lived in their basement! Bennie became "hysterical," promised to be good, and pleaded with his parents not to send him to the basement.

Sensing Bennie's intense fear, Mr. and Mrs. Meyers stopped threatening to put Bennie in the basement. They also told him that there was no dragon there.

Time-out should never be scary. A frightening place for time-out is likely to cause emotional problems in a child. The purpose of time-out is not to frighten a child, but to *bore* him.

Main Points To Remember:

1. A time-out place needs to be dull, boring, easily accessible, and *safe.*
2. Use a large straight-back chair for children between two and four.
3. Use a separate time-out room for children between five and twelve.
4. Never use your child's bedroom as a time-out place. Time-out won't work if you do.

Chapter 8

Explaining Time-Out
To Your Child

*"And when this timer rings you can come
out. . . ."*

Mom and Dad explaining time-out.

You and your spouse have selected a target behavior to be
decreased and have a boring place for time-out. Your next steps are
to explain time-out and to wait for the target behavior to occur.[56,62]
Introduce time-out when both you and your child are relaxed.
Also, be sure that both you and your spouse join together in describing time-out. Your child needs to know that you *both* expect him to
follow the rules in going to time-out and staying there until the timer
rings.

Tell your child that both of you love him, but that his behavior
of _____ is causing problems for him and the family. He
may quietly listen or he may want to argue when you tell him about
time-out. Don't argue with him and don't debate whether or not you
and your spouse have the right to put him in time-out.

The Two- To Four-Year-Old

If your child is between two and four, it's best to demonstrate and practice time-out in addition to explaining it.

Helping Melissa To Stop Biting

Melissa is three years old. When she gets angry with other children she both threatens to bite and actually bites. Mom, Dad, and Melissa are all sitting at the kitchen table.

Mother: *"Melissa, your Daddy and I both love you. We also want to help you. Remember yesterday when you got mad at James? You acted like you were going to bite him. Biting is against the rule."*

Melissa: *"Can I have a Coke?"*

Dad: *"Yes, in a couple of minutes. But right now we want to talk about biting and how to help you stop biting. If you bite or pretend to bite, you must sit on a chair. And you can't get down till this timer rings. When this timer rings you may get off the chair."*

Melissa: *"Can I have a Coke now?"*

Mother: *"In a minute. Let me show you what happens when you bite. (Mother picks up Melissa and sets her on a large chair in the corner of the kitchen.) When Mommie puts you here, you have to stay here. You can sit or kneel on the chair, but you can't stand up. And you can't get down or you will be in big trouble! You have to sit here until the timer rings. (Father rings the timer.) Did you hear the timer ring? That means you may get down now. (Mother lifts Melissa from the chair and places her on the floor.) That is time-out."*

Melissa: *"Are you going to get me a Coke now?"*

Mother: *"Yes, I will get you a Coke. But you remember—when you bite or pretend to bite someone, Mommie or Daddy will set you on a chair. You will have to stay there until the timer rings."*

Obviously, Melissa wasn't paying very close attention to her parents' explanation and demonstration of time-out. Melissa's parents will explain and demonstrate time-out two more times before actually using it. They could demonstrate time-out by using one of Melissa's dolls or stuffed animals.[68] Melissa will learn more about time-out, however, by actually experiencing it after she bites or threatens to bite.

The Five- To Twelve-Year-Old

The parents of an older child also need to introduce time-out to their child. Look at the following example of parents explaining time-out.

Telling Tim About Time-Out

Ten-year-old Tim has been hitting and threatening to hit his younger brother and other children when he gets angry wlth them. Other children are beginning to reject Tim because of his hitting and aggressiveness. Dad, Mom, and Tim are sitting around a small table.

Dad: *"Your Mom and I want to talk with you about the problem you've been having with hitting your brother and other kids when you get mad. We both love you, and we want to help you with this problem. Hitting is causing problems for you, your brother, and the whole family."*

Tim: *"Bobby starts it most of the time! I just hit him back when he hits me or calls me names."*

Mother: *"Yes, sometimes Bobby hits you and calls you names. Even though he is only five years old, he still needs to behave himself. We are going to have a talk with him, too. But now let's talk about you and time-out."*

Dad: *"Every time you hit or threaten to hit someone, your Mom or I will say time-out! That means that you must go to the bathroom immediately and stay there for 10 minutes. We will set this timer for 10 minutes. When you hear it ring, you may come out. You can't come out till it rings. If you don't go to time-out immediately or if you make a lot of noise in time-out, then you get extra minutes added on the timer. If you make a mess in time-out, then you get extra minutes on the timer and you have to clean up the mess before you come out."*

Tim: *"Who invented time-out anyway? What happens if I don't go to time-out? What happens if I leave time-out when I get ready?"*

Mother: *"Your Dad and I expect you to go to time-out and stay there till the timer rings. If you don't go, then no tele-*

> *vision and no bicycle for the rest of the day, until you go to time-out. Then you have to stay in time-out for 10 minutes plus one extra minute for every minute you delay going. You might have to stay as long as 15 minutes if you don't go right away or if you leave time-out before the timer rings. When your Dad and I tell you to go to time-out you must go! Your job is to go and stay there till the timer rings. Tim, do you have any questions about time-out?''*

Tim: *"Time-out is for little kids. It sounds silly. It sounds mean! Just spank me when I hit! And spank Bobby too. Will Bobby have to go to time-out?''*

Dad: *''If you hit each other, then you both have to go to time-out in separate places. Time-out will help you to stop hitting.''*

Mother: *"We love you and Bobby. We expect both of you to mind us. And when we tell you to go to time-out, you must go immediately.''*

When you tell your child about time-out, don't expect him or her to be enthusiastic about the plan. The next step for Tim's parents is to wait for the target behavior (hitting or threatening to hit) to occur.

When first beginning the time-out method, parents often wonder if their child will cooperate by going to time-out and by staying there until the timer rings. An uncooperative response to time-out usually isn't much of a problem. Appendix B, however, tells you what to do if you think your child might "rebel against time-out."

Main Points To Remember:
1. Mother and father both need to describe time-out to their child.
2. Tell your child that both of you love her and that you want to help her with a particular behavior problem.
3. Don't be surprised if your child acts annoyed or indifferent when you explain time-out.
4. Demonstrate time-out several times if your child is between two and four years old.

Chapter 9

Quickly Getting Your Child To Time-Out

"I don't want to go to time-out! I won't do it again! . . ."

Quickly *carry* your toddler to time-out.

This chapter will teach you the exact steps to follow in placing your child in time-out. It's important to get there *quickly!* Getting to time-out swiftly will reduce her resistance and will increase the effectiveness of this method of discipline. *You want your child to see an immediate connection between her bad behavior and the distasteful experience of time-out.*

By now, you have selected a boring place for time-out, explained time-out, and waited for the target behavior to occur. After your son or daughter displays the undesirable target behavior which you want to reduce, follow the basic steps described in the illustration, "Four Steps For Using Time-Out."

Four Steps For Using Time-Out
After The
Target Behavior Occurs

1. Send or place your child in time-out and use no more than 10 words and 10 seconds.

2. Get the portable timer, set it to ring in _____ minutes, and place it within hearing distance of your child. (Chapter 10)

3. Wait for the timer to ring—don't give your child any attention while he waits. (Chapter 10)

4. Ask your child, after the timer rings, why he was sent to time-out. (Chapter 11)

Follow the basic steps with all children between two and twelve. You may need to practice and gain experience before *automatically* following the steps. Many parents have a natural tendency to scold their child before placing her in time-out. However, this is a mistake. Scolding, arguing, and talking to a child before placing her in time-out encourage her to argue, become emotionally upset, and delay getting to time-out.

Many children try to avoid time-out by attempting to manipulate their parents. Children will protest, negotiate, blame another child, ask forgiveness, act indifferent, cry, plead, have a tantrum, or do something else to discourage you from sending them to time-out. Ignore all remarks and displays of emotion by your child. Remain calm and immediately place her in time-out. If she wants to talk with you, she may do so *after* time-out. *Be easy on yourself and your child; send her to time-out quickly. Use no more than 10 words and 10 seconds in doing so.* You'll find that time-out gets easier and easier when you use it correctly!

The Two- To Four-Year-Old

"For Spitting You Get Time-Out!"

Three-year-old Amanda was developing a bad habit of spitting or threatening to spit when angry with other children. Struggling with her sister over a toy, Amanda again introduced her effective weapon—spitting.

Mother immediately said, *"For spitting you get time-out!"* Quickly, Mother picked up Amanda from behind, walked across the room with her, and set her on a large straight-back chair. Amanda said, *"I don't want to go to time-out!" I won't do it again! . . ."* Unimpressed with her daughter's promise to stop spitting, Mother made no reply and simply left Amanda sitting on the time-out chair.

Good for Amanda's mother! She correctly followed the basic steps for placing her daughter in time-out. Carry two- and three-year-old children to the time-out chair. They are too young to quickly get there on their own. Some toddlers kick when carried to time-out, so be sure to carry them from behind. You can physically guide the four-year-old as she walks to a time-out chair. *Never* try to comfort or be affectionate with a child while you are taking her to time-out. Be stern or matter-of-fact and tell her, in 10 words or less, why she is being placed in time-out.

The Five- To Twelve-Year-Old

Older children are *sent* to time-out and must travel there on their own. *Develop the habit of giving effective commands when sending your child to time-out.* When his bad behavior occurs, walk near him, maintain a stern facial expression, and establish eye contact. Give a direct command to go to time-out and point in the direction of time-out. (Study the illustration of "Mother Handling Back-Talk.") Place the timer outside the door of the time-out room after your child arrives there.

Say only two things when placing your child in time-out.[24] *First,* label the misbehavior which your child demonstrated or state the rule he broke. Say, *"That was back-talk!"* or *"Hitting is against the rule!" Second,* command your child to go to time-out. Say, *"Go to time-out!"* or *"Go to time-out, immediately!"* Say nothing else. Now might be a good time to review the section in Chapter 2 on "How To Give Effective Commands."

Most children between the ages of five and twelve learn to obey a clear command to go to time-out. If you think that your child may refuse to go, study Appendix B—"If Your Child Rebels Against Time-Out." Appendix B will tell you how to handle any problems.

MOTHER HANDLING BACK-TALK

| 1. BACK-TALK | 2. TIME-OUT SIGN |

"I don't have to make my bed or clean my room. Why do I have to do it? You aren't doing anything!"

"Time-out for back-talk!"

3. POINTING TO TIME-OUT

"Go immediately to time-out!"

Use gestures to swiftly and effectively send the older child to time-out. *Point* in the direction of the time-out place while looking your child directly in the eye.

To signal the beginning of time-out, some parents use a "T" hand signal, the same time-out sign which is used in football.[30]

Be sure to limit yourself to no more than *10 words and 10 seconds* in sending your child to time-out.

The basic steps for using the time-out method are always the same regardless of what your child did to deserve time-out. To become effective at using time-out, follow the basic rules described in this book and gain experience by actually using this method.

When beginning the time-out method, it will be helpful to occasionally review various chapters of this book. Also, it will be helpful to discuss your time-out experiences and your child's reactions with your spouse or with another person who is interested in your child.

Main Points To Remember:
1. Place your child in time-out *quickly*—using no more than 10 words and 10 seconds.
2. *Carry* toddlers and preschoolers to the time-out chair.
3. *Send* the older child to the time-out place.

Chapter 10

The Timer And Waiting
In Time-Out

"IMPATIENTLY" WAITING FOR THE TIMER TO RING

*"Waaah! . . . I want down! . . . You're not my best friend!
. . . Bad, mean Daddy! . . . I want my Mommie! . . .
Doesn't anyone love me? . . . I don't like time-out . . .
Waaah!"*

It's upsetting to see your child angry and emotional.
What she says while in time-out may surprise or even
shock you. Be sure that you and your spouse give each
other lots of emotional support at these "difficult times."
After time-out is over, give her all the attention she
wants.

After placing your child in time-out, set the timer for _____
minutes, and place it within hearing distance of your child. She must
wait until she hears the timer ring before leaving time-out. Don't give
her any attention while the timer is ticking.

Deciding The Length Of Time-Out

Your child's age will determine how long she spends in time-out. In Chapter 6 you learned that children are to spend one minute in time-out for each year of age. If your child is two years old, always set the timer for two minutes each time that you place her in time-out. If she is twelve years old, set the timer for twelve minutes. *Don't place your child in time-out for longer than one minute for each year of age!*

Some parents who use *both* long and short periods of time-out find that the shorter periods of time-out become less effective. Do *not* use longer periods of time-out sometimes and shorter periods at other times. Parents often make the *mistake* of letting their anger toward their child's bad behavior determine how long their child will spend in time-out. Don't do this! Always use one minute for each year of age when placing your child in time-out. Only if your child *rebels* against time-out, should she spend more minutes in time-out than usual. Handling your child's possible resistance to time-out is discussed in Appendix B.

Where To Place The Timer

Place the timer out of reach, but within hearing distance of your child—about five to ten feet from the time-out place. The floor is a good spot for a timer. Your child will learn to listen for the timer to signal him when time-out is over. He will learn to depend on the timer rather than on your telling him when he may leave time-out. It's all right but not necessary that your child see the face of the timer. However, he should be able to hear it ticking and when it rings. Of course, never let a child handle or play with a timer *while* he is in time-out.

Toddlers and preschoolers, when they are *not* in time-out, often enjoy playing with a timer. Sometimes they put their dolls and toy animals on a time-out chair, next to a ticking timer. Allow them to practice their time-out skills because *someday* they, too, will be parents!

Why A Portable Timer Is Necessary

A timer helps a parent to be consistent, organized, and fair in using the time-out method of discipline. Place the portable timer near your child after placing him in time-out. *Do not use the timer on your kitchen stove.* You will always need to bring the timer to the time-out place. Your child must be able to actually hear the timer ring. *The timer determines when the child gets out of time-out and not the parent.* A portable timer helps to remove the time-out power struggle between parent and child. *Always use a portable timer.*[24,51,56,60]

DISCIPLINE *MISTAKES* PARENTS MAKE—
NOT USING A PORTABLE TIMER

"Mom, can I come out now? . . . Is the time up yet? . . ."

Your child will frequently call out to you if you don't use a portable timer. Failing to use a portable timer is a common mistake.

More reasons for using a portable timer:

- Timers can't be pestered and manipulated into ringing early.

- A timer doesn't forget to release a child from time-out. Parents sometimes do forget about a child in time-out.

- The child himself learns to take responsibility for leaving time-out at the proper time.

- A ticking timer is a sign to other family members that a child is in time-out. Anyone giving attention to a child in time-out also runs the risk of being placed in time-out.

- When a timer is used, children stop asking parents when they may come out of time-out. Parents get more peace and time to themselves while their child is waiting for the timer to ring. Timers are "parent savers."[60]

WAITING IN TIME-OUT

"I AM MAD! Mom shouldn't have sent me here. I didn't hit my little sister that hard. I hate time-out. I could try to force Mom and Dad to let me out of here. . . . I could scream as loud as I can— they hate that. . . . I could kick the door. . . . I could run water all over the floor. . . . or maybe I'll wait my 10 minutes and then watch television. . . ."

What The Parent Does During Time-Out

Remember that your main objective after placing your child in time-out is to avoid giving her any attention. Most parents need to remain in the same room when their two- or three-year-old is in time-out. After placing your toddler or preschooler on the time-out chair, "command" her to stay there and say nothing else. Turn your head away from her and avoid eye contact. If a preschooler has a tantrum on the time-out chair, some parents pretend to look at a newspaper or magazine in order to avoid giving their child any attention. Your child will recognize that you are ignoring him when he is in time-out.

If your child is between five and twelve years old, she will be in a *separate* room for time-out, and you will have some time by yourself. Think about the steps you used in placing your child in time-out. Did you follow the basic rules and steps? If your spouse or another person who cares for your child is present, this might be a good time to discuss your child's behavior and your skill in using the time-out method. However, your child shouldn't hear such a discussion, because it might be annoying to her and encourage her to rebel against time-out.

The parents of ten-year-old Justin asked him why he often screamed and became so emotional while in time-out. He replied, *"It feels good to let it all out . . . and I want you to feel as mad as I feel!"* Time-out was effective with Justin, but his parents sometimes had to give each other lots of emotional support during his time-outs!

When using time-out or any method of discipline, many parents begin to feel guilty, inadequate as parents, sorry for their child, or fear losing their child's love. Recognize that these feelings are natural for a parent and that all of us have doubts about our competence as parents. However, don't let these feelings prevent you from helping your child to improve his behavior. When you begin to seriously doubt yourself and feel significantly upset after disciplining your child, turn to Chapter 2 and read the section "Reasons Parents Don't Discipline Their Kids."

If your child rebels against the time-out method, then you need to study Chapter 12, "Common Mistakes Parents Make With Time-Out," and Appendix B, "If Your Child Rebels Against Time-Out." These two sections of *SOS!* will help you effectively handle your child's possible uncooperative response to the time-out method.

After the timer rings and time-out is over, what should you do or say to your child? Read on. The next chapter discusses this final time-out step.

Main Points To Remember:
1. The length of time-out is *one minute for each year of age.*
2. *Always use a portable timer. Don't* use the timer on your kitchen stove.
3. Place the timer out of reach but within hearing distance of your child.
4. Ignore your child until the timer rings.

Chapter 11

Talking With Your Child—
After Time-Out

AFTER TIME-OUT

*"I had to go to time-out because I hurt our
puppy. . . . Can I go outside and play now?"*

This chapter describes what you are to say to your child after
time-out is over. The chapter also discusses the appropriate time to
decide if additional punishment besides time-out is needed.

The Final Step In Using Time-Out

A Talk With Thomas—After Time-Out

Mother was reading her book when the timer near the
bathroom rang. Seven-year-old Thomas had been in time-out
for mistreating his puppy. With timer in hand, Thomas walks up
to his mother. Let's listen to their brief talk.

Mother: *"Hello Thomas. Tell me, why did you have to go to time-out?"*

Thomas: *"I had to go to time-out because I hurt our puppy. . . . Can I go out and play now? I want to ride my bike down to Mike's house."*

Mother: *"Yes, hurting the puppy was why you went to time-out. If you want to go to Mike's house, that's fine. Be back in about an hour though."*

Thomas: *"Okay, see you in about an hour. Good-bye."*

Mother correctly handled this brief "after time-out" discussion.

After your child hears the timer ring and leaves time-out, he should come to you. *He must tell you what he did or the rule he broke that caused him to be sent to time-out.* Some parents also have their child bring the timer as well.

If he tells you the correct reason why he was placed in time-out, acknowledge what he says with something like, "*Yes, _____ was why you had to go to time-out.*" That is all you should say. Normally, you shouldn't scold, make him say he is sorry, or have him promise to be good. He is free to go and usually neither of you will continue to be irritated.

If he doesn't remember why he was placed in time-out or gives you an incorrect reason, then *you* tell him why he was sent to time-out. After telling him the reason, say to him, *"Okay, I am going to ask you again. Tell me, why did you have to go to time-out?"* Continue this discussion until he can verbalize why you sent him to time-out. When this "after time-out" discussion is over, your child is free to go.

If your child is *two or three years old,* use the following plan when the timer rings. Say to him, *"The timer rang, you may get down now!"* Tell him, in a couple of words, the reason why he was placed in time-out. Ask him to repeat the reason. Then lift him from the chair and place him on the floor. Tell him he may go and play.

If your child is *four years old,* he will quickly learn to get off the chair by himself after hearing the timer ring. He also should tell you why he was placed in time-out.

In the "after time-out" discussion, parents sometimes learn that their child was actually "innocent" and didn't deserve to be put in time-out. When this happens to you, be sure to quickly apologize.

If your child remains annoyed after leaving time-out, ignore her annoyance. She has a right to her feelings. If she wants to talk about whether or not she should have been sent to time-out, listen to her. Avoid arguing with her, however.

Deciding *If* Additional Discipline Is Needed

Time-out immediately separates you and your child and gives both of you an opportunity to calm down. When used alone, time-out is normally enough punishment for bad behavior. You can avoid yelling, scolding, making ineffective threats and getting upset. You have used one of the most effective methods for stopping bad behavior which you could possibly use.

You may think that time-out is *not* sufficient punishment for a particular bad behavior. Perhaps another method of discipline should be used also. You should consider an additional method of discipline only *after* you have an opportunity to calm down. The time to make this decision is *while* your child is in time-out. Never announce an additional punishment *before* placing your child in time-out.

You may decide to use scolding, a natural or logical consequence, or behavior penalty in addition to time-out. These effective methods of mild discipline are discussed in Chapter 5. Usually, after your child is in time-out and you have a chance to "cool off," you'll decide that time-out used alone is sufficient. However, the correct time to decide if you need to use additional discipline is *after* placing your child in time-out.

Main Points To Remember:
1. After your child leaves time-out, he should tell you *why* he was sent to time-out.
2. When time-out is used alone, it is *usually* sufficient discipline for bad behavior.
3. The correct time to decide if additional discipline is needed is *while* your child is in time-out.

Chapter 12

Common *Mistakes* Parents Make With Time-Out

"Are you sorry for what you did? . . . Are you going to behave yourself when you come out? . . ."

Talking and arguing with a child *after* placing him in time-out is a *common mistake* which parents make.

The time-out method is easy to use, but it's also easy to make mistakes.[14,60] *This chapter describes nine common mistakes which parents often make when using time-out.* These mistakes reduce the effectiveness of time-out in changing the child's misbehavior. Be sure that *you* aren't making any of these mistakes.

Mistake #1   Talking or arguing with a child *after* placing him in time-out.

Correct Way—   *Ignore the child during time-out.*

Mistake #2	Talking or arguing with a child *before* placing him in time-out.
Correct Way—	*Use no more than 10 words and 10 seconds in quickly getting your child to time-out.*
Mistake #3	Using a small child's chair, rocking chair, or couch as a time-out place for toddlers and preschoolers.
Correct Way—	*Use a large straight-back chair as a time-out place for toddlers and preschoolers.*
Mistake #4	Using the child's bedroom or an interesting place for time-out with older children.
Correct Way—	*Use the bathroom or another boring place for time-out with older children.*

TIME-OUT *MISTAKES* PARENTS MAKE

"Dad forgot to use a timer."

Mistake #5	Keeping track of the time yourself or using a timer on the kitchen stove.
Correct Way—	*Always use a portable timer—and place it out of reach, but within hearing of the child.*

Mistake #6   Making a child apologize or promise to be good after he leaves time-out.

Correct Way—   *After leaving time-out, a child should tell her parent the misbehavior which caused her to be sent to time-out.* If the child doesn't remember, then the parent tells her what she did.

TIME-OUT *MISTAKES* PARENTS MAKE—
MERELY THREATENING TO USE TIME-OUT

"I've told you ten times to stay off the coffee table. If you get on the coffee table once more, you go to time-out! . . ."

Be sure to actually *use* time-out instead of *threatening* to use it. Merely threatening to use time-out is a common mistake.

Mistake #7   Threatening to use time-out instead of using it.

Correct Way—   *Actually use time-out each time the target behavior appears.* Don't just threaten to use it.

Mistake #8   Trying to shame or frighten a child with time-out.

Correct Way—   *Use time-out to bore a child and not to shame or*
                    frighten him.

Mistake #9   Using very long, very short, or different periods of
                    time for time-out.

Correct Way—   *Time-out lasts one minute for each year of age.*

Main Points To Remember:
1. Used correctly, the time-out method is effective and easy to use.
2. Used incorrectly, the time-out method is less effective and difficult
   to use.
3. Be sure that you are *not* making one of the *nine common time-out*
   mistakes.

Section Three

FURTHER APPLICATIONS OF YOUR PARENTING SKILLS

This section examines more methods for managing problem behavior. You'll learn how to use points, tokens, and parent-child contracts to improve a variety of behaviors. Steps for timing-out two children and for placing toys in time-out are discussed.

We'll study skills for managing bad behavior "away from home," handling aggressive and dangerous behavior, and using "reflective listening." Reflective listening helps children to express their feelings and emotions.

The final chapter looks at more childhood problems such as hyperactivity and resisting chores. (Is there any end to problems?) The chapter also teaches additional parenting skills such as "racing the timer" and using a "resting chair."

Let's look at these effective ways for helping children!

Chapter 13

Managing Bad Behavior
Away From Home

"Put it back! . . ."

"NO! I WANT IT!"

A child's obnoxious, demanding behavior *in public places* is embarrassing and difficult to handle.

When you and your child are away from home does his bad behavior ever embarrass you? Are you able to handle his loud complaining or persistent demands while visiting friends or shopping together? Do you ever think to yourself, *"I'll never take him anywhere again!"*

There is hope for you and your child! You can correct your child's embarrassing behavior in public. Use the methods described in this chapter and be more effective and confident when you and your child visit friends and relatives, shop, and go other places together.

To be an effective parent, you need to be a "well armed

parent"—equipped with a variety of sound discipline skills. Parents whose only discipline skill is "nagging and scolding" will do a *lot of that* on trips away from home with their child!

Begin with the parenting skills that you have already learned. Particularly important skills and methods include—frequently praising and commenting on good behavior and failing to reward bad behavior. Consider occasionally using logical consequences and behavior penalty, and sometimes employing time-out or variations of time-out. Glance back over the previous chapters to review some of these parenting skills.

A POCKET-SIZE TIMER

A pocket-size timer is convenient when visiting friends or traveling.

Visiting The Homes Of Friends And Relatives

Prepare your child for visits away from home. Ask her to take along several small toys or books to read. Be sure that she has something interesting to do while you're talking with adults. *Before leaving home, explain to your child the behavior which you expect.* Tell her the exact misbehavior (such as back-talk or angry screaming and screeching) which will result in time-out or in a particular behavior penalty (for example, no television later). If she behaves well, praise that behavior immediately or while you are returning home.

Use immediate time-out or "delayed time-out" to help manage misbehavior when you and your child are visiting. *Before you use time-out away from home, you should be comfortable and consistent when using it in your own home and when guests are present.*[27,66] In addition, your child should be cooperating with the time-out method, rather than rebelling against it.

When away from home, most parents choose to give their children *one* warning before sending them to time-out or telling them that they have "chalked up" a time-out. Just like you do at home, use one minute of time-out for each year of your child's age. Consider getting a pocket-size timer for trips away from home.

After you arrive at the home of relatives or friends notice any *dull, boring places* that you might use for time-out! Almost any place which is free of people and interesting activities will do.

PROBLEMS PARENTS FACE—OTHERS INTERFERE WITH DISCIPLINE

"SAVE ME, GRANDMA! Momma is going to put me in time-out! . . ."

Some relatives or friends may interfere when you attempt to discipline your child in their presence. Ask your spouse for emotional support and help in coping with these well-meaning relatives or friends.

Some parents successfully use the *backseat of their car as a time-out place* when they are away from home, especially if their child is usually *noisy* while in time-out.[27,66] After placing your child in the backseat, you sit in the front seat or stand outside the car. Be sure to ignore her and make sure that she doesn't have any toys while in time-out.

If possible, use an immediate time-out rather than a delayed time-out. Immediate time-outs are more effective in reducing bad behavior. When you can't send your child to time-out right away, then use delayed time-out.[2,51,62] *A child should go to delayed time-out directly after returning home.* Be sure that she goes to time-out immediately. *Delayed time-out should only be used with children who are four and older.*

Katie Almost Chalks Up A *Delayed Time-Out*

Seven-year-old Katie and her parents are visiting friends. It's after 10:00 p.m. and father *again* tells Katie that it's time to go home. Katie announces that she is *not* ready to leave yet and she backs up her announcement with whining, tears, and angry crying!

Father: *"Katie, ten minutes ago I told you it's time to go home. Go put your shoes and coat on now!"*

Katie: *"No, I don't want to go! I want to play some more! You never let me play when I want to! You always make me go home!"* (whining turns into loud crying).

Father: *"I am going to give you one warning. Stop crying and get your shoes and coat on right now—or it's time-out when you get home!"*

Katie: *"All right! You don't have to be so mean."* (Katie stops crying and puts on her shoes and coat.) *"Can we come back next week? I want to play some more."*

Father: *"We had a good time tonight. Yes, maybe all of us can get together next week."*

Father was effective in handling Katie's tantrum and refusal to return home. He *warned her once* and told her that if she didn't mind him, he would give her a *delayed time-out.*

Stores, Shopping Malls, And Restaurants

When getting ready for a shopping trip, be specific when telling your child how you want her to behave. When shopping, consider her age. Be reasonable about the length of time that you expect her to "tag along" without becoming tired, whining, and misbehaving.

If your child isn't tired, but simply acts like a "pest" while you are in a grocery store, shopping mall, or family restaurant, consider using a variation of time-out. In *grocery stores,* a good time-out place is usually in a corner or side aisle. Point to a safe spot on the floor for your child to sit. Turn your back, pretend "to look at groceries," and don't give her any attention. If she is very young, stand near her. If she is older, stand further away. But for safety's sake, always keep your child in sight.

At *shopping malls,* benches make excellent time-out places. Have your child sit on a bench. If your child is older, pick another bench for yourself. You'll both get a break from each other and an opportunity to rest! For time-out in *restaurants,* such as McDonald's, the older child can *briefly* sit alone at a separate table.

Most children who are in a public place will sit quietly while in time-out. However, if your child is crying loudly, select a time-out place outside the store, such as taking her to the backseat of your car. Or you may choose delayed time-out as an alternative.

"Be Quiet Or You Can't Play With Your Superman Suit!"

Twice each week my five-year-old son, Eric, accompanied my wife to the doctor's office where she got her allergy shots. Eric spent his time making noise and running in the waiting area. My wife spent her time trying to quiet him.

Finally my wife said, *"Eric, you are very noisy when we are at the doctor's office. Most of the people there are sick and waiting to see the doctor. In the future, each time that you run and are noisy, you won't be allowed to play with your Superman suit for the rest of the day."* Eric lost the privilege of playing with his Superman suit only one time. His favorite activity was playing with his Superman suit. After receiving *this* penalty, he immediately settled down. My wife rarely had difficulty with unruly behavior during their future visits to the doctor's office.

My wife was effective in reducing our son's bad behavior while they were away from home. She used the method of *behavior penalty*—in this case withdrawing a favorite activity or privilege.

When your child behaves badly in public, be sure that you don't accidentally reward and, consequently, strengthen that bad behavior. An example of rewarding bad behavior is allowing your daughter to keep the candy bar she grabbed while standing in the check-out line. To quickly return home because your child has a temper tantrum is another instance of rewarding bad behavior. However, remember that young children tire easily. Don't make the shopping trip too long.

Reward your child if she behaves while you are shopping. Give her praise or let her get a piece of gum from the gum dispenser as you *leave* the grocery store, *but only if she has been good.* Before leaving the department store, let her look at something that she had wanted to see, such as the animals in the pet department or the dolls in the toy department.

In The Car

A miserable experience for parents is to ride in a car with a backseat of noisy, fighting children. Help prevent bad behavior by carefully organizing the car as well as the trip. Be sure that everyone (you, too!) wears a seat belt. Wearing seat belts reduces behavior problems. Seat belts prevent children from crowding too close together and invading each other's "space." The trip is not only more pleasant, but safer for everyone. On long trips, one parent might sit in the backseat to keep the children from "roughhousing" or annoying each other. Ask your children to select toys, books, or a game to take in the car.

Before leaving on a car trip, you can often anticipate the likelihood of misbehavior occurring. If you suspect problems, tell your children in advance that a particular consequence will occur if they misbehave in the car. Also, tell them that they will get only one warning before receiving a consequence. An appropriate consequence could be a *delayed time-out* or a mild *behavior penalty such as stopping the car* for several minutes until the misbehavior ends. Pulling the car off the road for five or ten minutes is more effective if you are traveling somewhere appealing to children—such as the beach or a park.

When a child gets a *delayed time-out,* she must go to time-out as soon as possible, usually as soon as you return home. However, on a long car trip, she should do her time-out as soon as you stop at a rest area along the highway. She briefly stays in the car for her time-out after the rest of the family leave the car. A parent should stay near the car.

Outdoor Play Activities

At the park, zoo, swimming pool, and on camping trips, it's easy to use *immediate time-out* to manage your child's misbehavior. Point to a *safe place* for your child to sit—on a park bench, on a large rock, by a tree, at the corner of the playground, or in the backseat of your car.[66] Immediate time-out is easy to use and it's effective when parents follow through with it.

One mother was amazed because *immediate time-out* worked so well in controlling the "brat behavior" of her nine-year-old son while they were at the swimming pool. After receiving two immediate time-outs, he stopped splashing and dunking younger children. His behavior toward the other children improved and his mother's relationship with the other mothers greatly improved! Previously, she had tried scolding and yelling, but these methods were completely ineffective. In fact, he made faces at her when she scolded him. She considered taking him home if he misbehaved (a logical consequence), but this would punish her too! Time-out was a mild consequence, but it was completely effective in eliminating her son's misbehavior.

If your child misbehaves near your house or apartment, it isn't necessary to have him come indoors for time-out. Have him sit some specific place such as the front steps. Place the timer within hearing distance. After the timer rings, he should return it to you.

Main Points To Remember:
1. Effective parents equip themselves with a variety of sound discipline skills and don't rely solely on scolding and nagging.
2. Be sure to frequently reward your child's good behavior with attention and praise. Do this at home *and* away from home.
3. In the home of friends, use time-out as you do in your own home.
4. In public places, consider using *immediate time-out, delayed time-out,* or *behavior penalty.*

Chapter 14

Using Points, Tokens, And Contracts

"Let's see. You get one point for straightening your room and one point for clearing the table after supper. I'm really proud that you earned these points! . . ."

Children enjoy working for points. When Susan gets enough points, she will exchange them for a small doll.

A Point-Reward Program Helps Susan

Seven-year-old Susan had several problem behaviors which bothered her parents. She often left clothes, toys, and books scattered about her room. Mr. and Mrs. Madison tried letting her "live in the clutter" (a natural consequence) but that didn't bother Susan a bit. She seemed to enjoy the mess.

When asked to help with simple chores, Susan often complained, said that she was *"too tired,"* or whined that *"Chores aren't any fun."* Her parents tried nagging and scolding. However, Susan continued resisting their requests.

Although frustrated, Susan's parents began a special reward program and within two weeks Susan's behavior greatly improved. How did Mr. and Mrs. Madison help their daughter to change? They used a point-reward program! Read on to see how they developed this program.

Material rewards (a small toy) and activity rewards (going to the park) help motivate children to improve their behavior. Provide a way for your child to earn tokens, points, or check marks in order to purchase rewards. After earning a number of points or tokens, your child can exchange them for a particular reward that she wants.

Earning "tokens" motivates adults as well as children. If you have a job outside your home, you earn "tokens" (in the form of paychecks and money) which you exchange for material rewards (a pizza, new shoes) and activity rewards (going to the movies or on vacation). To help your child develop a new behavior or habit, you sometimes need to offer her more than praise and attention. Once her new behavior is well established, you can "phase out" and eventually discontinue this special incentive program.

Parents can use *token rewards* with children who are four or five years old. *Point-rewards* are effective with children six to twelve. *Parent-child contracts,* another type of special incentive plan, are used with children from seven or eight through adolescence. Let's look closer at these special programs.

Offering Point-Rewards

Follow six steps in putting together an effective point-reward program for your child:

1. Select a target behavior.
2. Make a point-reward calendar.
3. Write a "menu of rewards."
4. Keep track of the points earned and spent.
5. Adjust the reward program.
6. Discontinue the program.

1. Select one or more target behaviors that you want improved. You must be able to pinpoint and actually count the behavior that you want increased such as clearing the table after meals.

Describe the target behavior in positive rather than negative terms. For example, Mr. and Mrs. Madison asked Susan to "have a clean bedroom" rather than to "stop having a messy bedroom." They also listed several other behaviors such as emptying the trash, regularly brushing her teeth, etc.

2. Make a "point-reward calendar." Write down the target behaviors on this calendar. Also, write down the time when you will check to see if the behavior has occurred or not. Next to each target behavior, list one or more points that your child might earn for that behavior.

Susan's Point-Reward Calendar

For Improving *Several* Behaviors

POINTS EARNED							
List of Good Behaviors (and possible points)	**S**	**M**	**T**	**W**	**T**	**F**	**S**
Clean bedroom, check at 6:00 pm (2 points)	0	//	//				
Clear dinner table (each meal, 1 point)	/	//	//				
Empty trash by 6:00 pm (1 point)	/	0	/				
Brush teeth (each meal, 1 point)	//	/	///				
Be home on time after school (2 points)	0	0	//				
Tantrum-free day (2 points)	0	0	//				
TOTAL POINTS EARNED	////	//// /	//// //// ////				

This calendar provides a record of *several* behaviors for *one week*. Post a new calendar each week.

At the end of each day, total the number of points your child has earned. Draw marks through points on the bottom line when your child spends those points.

Examine the point-reward calendar which Mr. and Mrs. Madison made for Susan. They designed a calendar for recording several behaviors at one time. However, it's usually easier for parents to learn how to use a point-reward program by first focusing on only one problem behavior. Study the "Point-Reward Calendar For Improving *One* Behavior."

After you prepare a calendar, post it in a conspicuous place. Most parents tape it to the refrigerator door or place it on a bulletin board.

3. Write down a "menu of rewards" and post it near the point-reward calendar.[24] A "menu of rewards" is a list of small material rewards and activity rewards (privileges) which your child desires. Ask her what she would like to work for. Susan said that she wanted to work for a comic book, a particular doll, a trip to McDonald's, etc.

Point-Reward Calendar
For Improving *One* Behavior

POINTS EARNED							
Good Behavior (and possible points): *Room is neat. This means bed is made and all clothes, toys, and books are put in their proper places. Check at 7:30 a.m. (1 point). Check at 6:00 p.m. (1 point).*							
	S	**M**	**T**	**W**	**T**	**F**	**S**
First Week	0	/	0	//	/	//	//
Second Week	//	//					
Third Week							

This calendar records *one* behavior for *several* weeks. At the end of the third week, post a new calendar.

When your child spends a point, draw a red mark or slash through that point. Points without slash marks are points not yet spent. Encourage your child to spend her points rather than save them.

After you and your child list possible rewards, then *you* decide how many points each reward will "cost." You don't want the rewards to be too easy or too hard to earn because your daughter might lose enthusiasm for the program. After you gain experience using a menu of rewards, it will be easier to determine the appropriate cost for new rewards. It's best to begin a point-reward program using small rewards which don't cost your child very much (and don't cost you very much!) so that she has the opportunity to *frequently* earn rewards.

Sample "Menu Of Rewards"

Menu of Rewards	
Reward	**Cost in Points**
Comic book	4
Trip to McDonald's	12
Dad plays ping-pong with me	4
Soft drink from refrigerator	6
Package of sugarless gum	3
Make popcorn	9
Staying up till 9:30 p.m. on school night	7
Trip to park	8
Ice cream bar from freezer	6
Play cards with mother	4
Trip to get pizza	15
Small doll (less than $7.00)	30

This "menu" lists various material rewards and activity rewards.[24] It also lists how many points (or tokens) your child must pay for each reward. Post this menu next to the point-reward calendar.

4. Keep track of the points as your child earns and spends them. When your child earns a point, record it on the calendar with enthusiasm. Give lots of praise for her good behavior and the points she earns.

Encourage her to spend her points rather than save them so that she will enjoy the program more. After she spends a point and receives a reward, place a slash mark through that point.

When your child has earned enough points to select a reward, let her purchase the reward as soon as possible. If she is as young as six or seven, be particularly quick to help her exchange points for a reward.

5. Make adjustments within the program so that it works better. Keep the old calendars after posting new ones. By looking at these old calendars, both of you can see how much progress she has made in improving her behavior.

The calendars tell you how well your program is working. To improve the program, make clearer definitions of what she must do to earn points and add new rewards to the menu. Be sure that you give her these rewards only if she earns them. If she gets rewards without working for them, why should she work?

Some parents use *fines* for bad behavior—they take away points that their child has earned. However, children get discouraged with the program if they lose points after earning them. Combine other methods of discipline for bad behavior, such as logical consequences or time-out, with the point-reward program for *good* behavior. For example, Susan's parents placed her in time-out when she had a tantrum. When she had a *tantrum-free day,* she earned two points. Her tantrums rapidly decreased.

6. Phase out the program. Don't keep a point-reward program indefinitely, just until your child's behavior improves. Tell your child that the point-rewards helped her to make improvements in her behavior and that you are proud of these improvements. Continue to praise her improved behavior and discontinue the point-reward program. There are several ways that parents can phase out the program.[68] Omit giving points when she fails to ask for them. Increase the amount of time between earning the points and exchanging them for rewards. Consider having a party for her since she has "graduated" from the program.[24] Take her and the family to a special place to eat that she has chosen.

Giving Token Rewards

A clear plastic container is a good place for
young children to keep their tokens.

Most four- and five-year-olds prefer to earn tokens rather than points because they can touch and hold tokens and carry them around. Use poker chips, marbles, play money, or other small objects as tokens. Don't let your child handle or play with any tokens unless she has earned them. She will need a container, perhaps a plastic jar or cup, for her tokens. If she is four or five, encourage her to keep the token container in a special place so she won't lose her tokens.

You need to select a target behavior and make up a menu of rewards. Give your child tokens rather than points for her good behavior. For preschoolers, draw or cut out pictures of rewards (a toy, an ice cream bar) for the menu of rewards. Next to the picture of each reward, draw another picture showing the number of tokens she must pay for that reward.

When the target behavior occurs, give your child a token. When she has earned enough tokens, she can purchase a reward. A token-reward program is simple to operate once it's set up and after your child learns that she can exchange tokens for "goodies."

Tokens And Ice Cream Bars

Four-year-old Ann rarely answered or came when her mother called her. Mother decided to use a token-reward program and to give Ann a token each time that Ann *came when called.* Ann said that she wanted to work just for ice cream bars in the freezer. Mother said that each ice cream bar would cost five tokens.

Ann earned one or two ice cream bars a day for a week. Mother then slowly discontinued the token-reward program. However, Ann's improved behavior of *coming when called* continued.

Writing Parent-Child Contracts[17,37,56,76]

"He's Lonely By Himself"

"He's lonely out there all by himself," eight-year-old Paul pleaded. *"He gets cold in the garage. See, he always tries to make a nest to keep warm. I want him in my room."*

Mrs. Carr had been listening to these same insistent, monotonous statements from Paul for the past two weeks. She was tired of hearing Paul say that he wanted his gerbil in his room. She felt sorry because Paul and his gerbil were separated. However, she knew that she would also get tired of cleaning up after the gerbil if Paul moved it inside the house.

Paul's father suggested that the three of them write up an agreement spelling out Paul's responsibilities for keeping the gerbil's cage clean. Mr. Carr said that the contract should also state the consequences if Paul didn't keep his part of the bargain. If Paul didn't regularly clean the cage, then the gerbil would be returned to the garage.

A contract was written, dated, and signed by all three
family members. The Carr family discovered a new way for
handling family disagreements—parent-child contracts.

PARENT-CHILD CONTRACTS—
SOMETIMES AN EFFECTIVE SOLUTION

*"I'll do it. I'll clean his cage every week. And
you and Mom will let me keep him in my room.
Let's all sign the contract now! . . ."*

*A parent-child contract is a written agreement between parent
and child.* All parties join together in identifying a problem, discussing and negotiating a solution, clarifying responsibilities, signing the
agreement, and following through with the agreement.

Contracts are used with children as young as seven or eight.
These problem solving tools are especially useful to families with
adolescents.

Think of a problem that your family has. Consider "negotiating"
a parent-child contract to resolve it.

Follow four steps in writing and using a contract:

1. Identify a problem.

2. Negotiate a solution with your child.

3. Write down the agreement.

4. Sign the contract and follow it.

1. Identify a problem. Contracts usually focus on resolving *a single problem* concerning a family, such as Paul keeping a gerbil in his room. Contracts are successfully used to encourage children to come home promptly after school and to set a time for doing homework each day. Negotiate a contract with your child *before* he gets a new pet. It's important to negotiate a contract *before* he receives a potentially hazardous object such as a BB gun, archery equipment, or a chemistry set. The contract should state that he will temporarily lose the object if he becomes careless with it.

Completed Parent-Child Contract

```
┌─────────────────────────────────────────────────────────────┐
│                         CONTRACT                            │
│                                                             │
│  I,     Paul    , agree to:  (1) Clean my gerbil's cage     │
│        (child's name)                                       │
│  each Saturday. (2) Vacuum around the cage each             │
│  Saturday.                                                  │
│                                                             │
│                                                             │
│                                                             │
│  We, Mother and Father, agree to: Allow Paul to keep        │
│  the gerbil in his bedroom. If cage and surrounding         │
│  area aren't cleaned each Saturday, then gerbil goes        │
│  back to the garage.                                        │
│                                                             │
│                                                             │
│  Date contract begins:      5/13/8-                         │
│  Date contract ends:        Contract continues as long as   │
│                             gerbil is in Paul's room.       │
│                                                             │
│  Date contract signed:      5/13/8-                         │
│  Agreed to by:              Paul                            │
│                             (Child's signature)             │
│                             Mother                          │
│                             (Mother)                        │
│                             Father                          │
│                             (Father)                        │
└─────────────────────────────────────────────────────────────┘
```

Contracts help families by clarifying agreements and responsibilities. If Paul doesn't clean his gerbil's cage each week as agreed, then the gerbil must be returned to the garage.

Contracts have been used with adolescents to encourage regular attendance at school and to set a deadline for returning home after dates. *Before* your son or daughter begins using the family car, negotiate and sign a contract stating his or her responsibilities.

See Chapter 20 for examples of how a written agreement between child, teacher, and parent can improve a child's school progress or adjustment at school.

2. Negotiate a solution with your child. Try to jointly agree on a solution rather than forcing one on him. The older your child, the more real power or authority you should let *him* have in helping to figure out a solution. Don't impose a contract on an adolescent. If you do, he may rebel and intensify family conflict.

Be sure that your spouse stays involved throughout the negotiations. Sometimes, busy husbands try to shift negotiating responsibilities to their wives. Or a harried wife may dump the responsibility on her husband when he arrives home. Choose a time when everyone is relatively calm. Be patient, positive, and stay focused on the actual behavior or actions which you want to occur.

Before my family subscribed to cable television, we all spent considerable time discussing potential problems and solutions. My wife and I were concerned that our boys would watch too much television or watch programs oriented toward sex and violence. After several weeks of negotiations, the four of us signed a contract. That contract helped prevent a lot of family disagreements.

3. Write down the negotiated agreement. The contract should state what *you* agree to do and what *your child* agrees to do. State the consequences if the parties don't comply with the agreement. Include a date when the contract ends or is to be renegotiated.

The contract should be fair to all. Everyone should be gaining something as well as giving up something. It states what each person is to do and what he is to receive in return. Consider the contract which Mr. and Mrs. Carr negotiated with their son, Paul.

4. Sign the contract, post it, and follow through with your responsibilties. After everyone signs the contract, post it on a bulletin board or put it where everyone can find it. If your child says that a *posted* contract embarrasses him in front of his friends, keep the contract in a special folder.

If your child doesn't fulfill his responsibilities, then follow the consequences which are written into the contract. Most families who use contracts say that they're great tools for preventing and solving problems.

Main Points To Remember:

1. *Point-rewards and tokens* motivate children to improve a wide variety of problem behaviors.

2. Children select tangible rewards and privileges from a *menu of rewards,* after earning points or tokens.
3. *Parent-child contracts* help solve family problems, especially disagreements between parents and older children.

Chapter 15

Timing-Out Two Children

Fights between brothers and sisters are common problems which parents face.

When *two* children misbehave, it isn't always necessary to know who started the problem or who is mostly at fault. Just send both children to time-out, in separate time-out places.

In this chapter, you'll learn *why* timing-out two children is an effective method for handling problems *between* children. The chapter also discusses *when and how* to use "time-out for two."[60] This method is generally most effective when used with children who are at least three or four years old.

Reducing Conflict *Between* Children

Time-Out For Two

Ten-year-old Andrew and nine-year-old Angela were "making faces" and calling each other names. Since father believed that Andrew had started the conflict, father placed only Andrew in time-out.

Andrew was now returning from time-out and father overheard *another* argument beginning between Andrew and his sister.

Angela: *"You had to go to time-out, Andrew! Ha,ha,ha! Dad is on my side and he put you in time-out!"*

Andrew: *"Shut up! You know that you started calling me names first. Do you want to get a fat lip?"*

Angela: *"Ha! Just try it! You are a big baby and you are always starting fights around here and Mom and Dad know it!"*

At this moment father walks up, annoyed with both children.

Father: *"Time-out for fighting! Angela, you in the bathroom! Andrew—the back bedroom! Go!!"*

Good for father! He is recognizing that it takes two to fight. Also, he is beginning to realize that "time-out for two" often is more effective than punishing only *one* child or personally solving persistent problems between his children.

Name calling, using threatening gestures, loud arguing, hostile teasing, and hitting are common behavior problems which parents face. By acting as a judge or referee, parents sometimes take too much responsibility for solving problems *between* their children. Too frequently, parents intervene and attempt to determine which child started the disagreement in order to blame and scold the guilty child. Consequently, the children become overly dependent on parents to settle problems rather than resolving their own problems. And the possibility always exists that the parent may "judge" incorrectly.

Many children delight in getting a brother or sister into trouble. A "clever" child may begin an argument but make it appear as if the other child started the conflict. Sometimes, a younger child who appears helpless or "innocent" actually provokes an older child into harassing him. When children have disagreements and arguments, it's frequently difficult to say who started the conflict.

Children love getting attention from their parents. Your children may be learning to get considerable attention from you by constantly arguing and fussing with each other. Of course you dislike hearing and seeing conflict between your children. However, if you step in and handle the disagreement yourself, you may be "accidentally" rewarding one or both of your children for continuously arguing.

What should you do as a parent? When two children are arguing and fighting with each other, consider sending both children to time-out. *There are three advantages for timing-out both children. First,* you don't have to take sides or determine which child is "mostly at fault." *Second,* you don't accidentally reward them with lots of attention while you settle their arguments. *Third,* both children are discouraged from continuing their conflicts because both receive the same boring and unpleasant experience of time-out.

When And How To Use "Time-Out For Two"

Time-out for two is effective for handling problems *between* children as discussed above. Another appropriate time to use time-out for two is when your children get into trouble *together,* even though they may be getting along fine with each other. Let's assume that, despite several scoldings, your children continue chasing each other through the house, playing tag, and slamming doors. This would be a suitable time to place both children in time-out.

Look over the list of *"Misbehaviors Which Deserve Time-Out"* in Chapter 4, "What Is Time-Out? When Do Parents Use It?" Time-out for two would be fitting for almost all of these behaviors if both children are involved in these misbehaviors together.

Prior to using time-out for two, you should be experienced in timing-out each of the children individually. Before actually placing two children in time-out, wait for the moment when *both* children are misbehaving. Then immediately tell both of them to go to time-out, but to different time-out places. Be sure that no one takes any toys to time-out and that they can't see each other from their separate time-out places. Place the timer where each child can hear it ring. (Of course, more than two children may be timed-out if each has experienced time-out on previous occasions.)

How long should the children be in time-out if they are, for example, six and ten years old? Set the timer for eight minutes since their average age is eight.

Be sure to give your children attention and special privileges when they behave and get along with each other. One mother of two young children, after experiencing a pleasant morning at home, said, *"You two are playing so well with each other this morning. Let's go to the park this afternoon! It's easy to go places together when you get along so well!"*

Main Points To Remember:
1. Since it takes two to fight, consider using *time-out for two.*

2. Timing-out two children has some distinct advantages over other methods of handling persistent problems *between* children.
3. Follow the same steps for timing-out two or more children as timing-out one child. Send them to separate time-out places.
4. When your children are behaving themselves and getting along with each other, be sure to reward them with lots of attention and praise.

Chapter 16

Timing-Out A Toy
Instead Of The Child

PROBLEMS PARENTS FACE

TIMING-OUT A TOY—
AN EFFECTIVE SOLUTION

"It's mine!"

"NO! IT'S MINE!"

Toys often cause problems between children. Sometimes children hit others with toys, damage furniture with toys, or refuse to share toys.

"We better share next time. If we don't share, nobody will get to play with it again. Dad will put our toy back in time-out. . . ."

In the future, Jeffrey and Lisa will be less likely to fight over a toy. They will be more likely to share it.

This chapter describes a useful variation of time-out called "timing-out a toy instead of the child."* You will learn the correct

---

*When a toy or another object is placed in "time-out," the child briefly loses the privilege of playing with that object.[14] This time-out procedure, which follows a child's misbehavior with an object, might also be called a logical consequence or behavior penalty. These two methods of discipline are discussed in Chapter 5.

steps for easily using this effective method of discipline. Other skills discussed in this chapter include *using a timer to take turns* and *placing personal belongings in a "Sunday Box"* if they are left scattered about the house.

Timing-Out The Robot *Instead* Of The Children

Last night father enjoyed bringing home a toy robot for five-year-old Jeffrey and six-year-old Lisa. This morning he reluctantly spent most of his time deciding "who had the toy first," insisting that both children take turns, and scolding them for arguing with each other.

In order to stop the nearly continuous squabbling, father finally decided to put *the toy robot* in time-out. He placed the robot on top of the refrigerator, set the portable timer for ten minutes, and put the ticking timer next to the robot. He then turned to his children and said, *"After the timer rings, I will get the robot down for you. However, if you two continue having problems sharing the toy, then it will go back into time-out!"*

The robot didn't have to go back into time-out that morning because Jeffrey and Lisa learned to share their new toy rather than having it put in time-out. They each learned that they would *lose* the fun of playing with their new toy if they continued fighting over it.

Timing-Out Toys And Stopping Misbehavior

Children spend an enormous amount of time playing with toys and other objects. Toys provide a way for children to socialize with other children and with their parents.[13] You can help children to learn increased self-control and how to share, when they play with toys and with each other.

Consider "timing-out a toy" instead of using some other method of discipline. There are at least three situations when you might choose to use this new method of discipline—(1) Your child misbehaves while playing with a toy (such as damaging furniture with a toy); (2) Two children misbehave and their misbehavior involves a toy (playing catch with an expensive toy not intended to be thrown); and (3) Two children argue and fuss over a toy rather than sharing it.

When your child invites a friend over to play and the misbehavior of the two children involves a toy, you might consider timing-out the toy. The parents of the other child couldn't object to your placing a toy in time-out—although they might be puzzled by this procedure! Timing-out a toy is an ideal method of discipline for use by adults who are responsible for several children at one time, such as preschool teachers and day-care workers.

You may be wondering, "Why should parents time-out a toy instead of their child?" You don't want children spending too much time in time-out. A child who is in time-out loses the opportunity to learn new things and to try new behavior which might be rewarding or enjoyable. Also, *when you use discipline you should use the mildest possible form which is still effective in changing behavior.* Timing-out a toy is a milder punishment than timing-out the child. Timing-out a toy gives you an effective alternative to timing-out your child and an additional way to "back up" your warnings.

When two children repeatedly fuss over a toy, don't be overly concerned with finding out which child is at fault or which child should be blamed for the argument. *Avoid taking sides.* Simply place the toy or object in time-out. That way neither child will be rewarded for arguing and fussing. Also, after the two "combatants" lose their toy to time-out, they will be more highly motivated in the future to work out their own problems.

Steps For Timing-Out Toys

What steps do you take when timing-out a toy or another object? When your child misbehaves with a toy, quickly remove the toy and place it in time-out. Use no more than ten words and ten seconds *before* placing the toy in time-out. *After* timing-out the toy, tell your child why it had to go to time-out. Then ask *him* to state aloud why the object was placed in time-out. Be brief and avoid scolding.

Don't require your child to place a toy in time-out himself. You can do it much quicker and also avoid a possible power struggle. Always use a portable timer. It will signal your child when he may resume playing with a toy. The reasons for using a portable timer when timing-out toys are essentially the same as for timing-out children. Review "More Reasons For Using A Portable Timer" in Chapter 10.

For children who are *two or three years old,* place the toy out of the child's reach or where it can be easily observed by you. Next, get the portable timer and set it for a short period of time, usually two to five minutes. Place the ticking timer next to the toy so that your child sees the toy and timer together. Then briefly tell him why the toy went to time-out. For example say, *"You hit the coffee table with your toy. That is why I put your toy in time-out."* Next, tell him that the toy can leave time-out as soon as the timer rings. When the timer rings, again briefly tell him why the toy had to go to time-out and then hand it to him. Normally, you shouldn't ask him to apologize for his bad behavior or make him promise to be good in the future.

For children who are *four and older,* it's usually not necessary to place the toy out of the child's reach. Simply say, *"Time-out for* (give

Timing-Out Toys And Other Objects:
A Solution To Persistent Problems—
Examples For Parents

Problem Behavior	A Solution*
1. Two sisters, ten and thirteen years old, continue squabbling with each other about which television program to watch. They repeatedly complain to mother and want *her* to solve *their* problem.	1. Mother turns off the television, sets a timer for ten minutes, and places the timer on the television set. (She should repeat the procedure if necessary.)
2. Four-year-old Alan repeatedly rides his Big Wheel vehicle too near the street after being told not to do so by father.	2. Father puts the Big Wheel in a time-out place inside the garage for twenty minutes.
3. Six-year-old Andrea plays "catch" with her pet hamster.	3. The hamster is placed back in its cage and can't come out for the rest of the day.
4. Daniel and his friend, both four years old, knock over each other's blocks and threaten to throw them at each other.	4. Daniel's mother sets a timer for ten minutes and places it next to the pile of building blocks. Mother also explains time-out to Daniel's surprised friend.
5. Erin repeatedly complains that her brother won't take turns with their new video game.	5. Father turns off the video game and sets the timer for ten minutes. (He may need to repeat this a couple of times.)
6. The stereo in the living room is "vibrating" the apartment again.	6. The stereo is turned off, and the portable timer is set for fifteen minutes and placed on the stereo.

*Parents, of course, must decide which behavior problems are serious enough to warrant a mild punishment such as timing-out a toy. There are ways of handling the above problems other than using time-out. However, timing-out a toy is quick, effective, and easy for parents to use.

name of object)! *Don't touch it!"* Get the timer, set it for ten to fifteen minutes, and place the timer next to the toy. Then tell your child why you placed the toy in time-out. Tell him that he may retrieve the toy from time-out after he hears the timer ring. No one touches a ticking timer or an object in time-out. If they do, then they get to go to time-out themselves! Even impulsive children quickly learn to control themselves and to wait for the timer to ring before removing a toy from time-out.

More Ideas For Parents

Help your children to *practice taking turns by using a timer.* Timers keep accurate track of the time and are fair to each child.

For example, if two children have trouble sharing a new video game, sit down with them and have them practice the desirable behavior (taking turns). Have each child set the timer for five minutes and play the video game until the timer rings. Then, the child playing the game immediately must give up the game and hand it to the other child. The other child sets the timer for five minutes and begins his turn.

Continue helping them to practice setting the timer and taking turns until you are sure both children know the procedure. However, if they choose to continue squabbling over the video game rather than sharing it, then place the video game in time-out. This will motivate each of them to cooperate.

It's often difficult to get children to pick up their toys, shoes, clothes, records, and other objects which they leave on the floor and scattered about the house. *Use a "Sunday Box" for out-of-place personal belongings.*[2,44,51]

Place a cardboard box, marked "Sunday Box," in the living room or in any other room which you want cleared of clutter. Set a timer for ten minutes and place it next to the box. Then announce to your family that you are putting all out-of-place belongings in the box when the timer rings. The objects are kept there until Sunday, when you release them to their owners. Give no further warning and do not scold. After the timer rings, pick up all out-of-place objects, place them in the box, and place the box in a closet. No one touches the objects or the Sunday Box until Sunday. After losing their toys and other objects several times, children will pick up their own belongings and you won't have to scold and nag.

When you see two *toddlers or preschoolers* arguing and fussing over a toy, consider using *distraction.* Draw their attention or redirect their interest to a new toy or activity. One or both children will usually give up the old toy or activity and try the new activity. Consequently, they have another opportunity to play cooperatively or apart from each other. Most young children can be easily distracted.

When your child plays well with others, reward him with your praise, approval, and attention. Young children need *encouragement,* and they love *words of praise for their good behavior.*

Main Points To Remember:
1. When your children's misbehavior involves a toy, consider removing the toy and placing the toy in time-out.
2. *Timing-out toys* and other objects gives the parent an effective alternative to timing-out the child.
3. Help your children *practice setting the timer and taking turns* with a toy or activity.
4. Consider using a *Sunday Box* for out-of-place belongings.

Chapter 17

Handling Aggressive And Dangerous Behavior

"Help! Help!"

Dangerous behavior must be handled immediately. After stopping the behavior, use several methods of effective discipline.

"I Was Just Going To Scare Him With It!"

Early one Saturday morning, while straightening my garage, I heard two desperate cries, *"Help! Help!"* My five-year-old son, Eric, was holding a bat and chasing Cory, our six-year-old neighbor. Cory was obviously terrified and "running for his life." Considering the situation, Cory's emotional state and behavior were appropriate!

Running out the garage door, I shouted, *"Stop swinging that bat! No hitting!"* I grabbed the bat, saying, *"Don't ever chase anyone with a bat!"* Next, I gave Eric several sharp swats on his bottom and said, *"Time-out! Go sit on those porch steps, NOW!"* Eric walked off to time-out, holding his bottom with both hands.

I turned to check on Cory, but he had disappeared, apparently running off to "safety." Next, I looked at the bat and was somewhat relieved to find that it was a hollow plastic bat used for hitting plastic balls.

After Eric's time-out was over, we had the following talk:

Father: *"Eric, never try to hit someone with a bat or with any object! It's dangerous and will hurt someone badly."*

Eric: *"I wasn't really going to hit Cory with the bat. I was just going to scare him with it!"*

Father: *"Never use an object for hitting or scaring someone! Eric, tell me again. What did you do that was dangerous?"*

Eric: *"I chased Cory with a bat. He wouldn't take turns hitting the ball."*

Father: *"Chasing Cory with a bat was dangerous and wrong. Tell me, what can you do next time if Cory won't take turns, and you get mad? What can you do that is safe? You tell me."*

Eric: *"Well, I could tell him that I won't play with him if he doesn't take turns. . . . I could tell his mother on him . . . I could come and tell you that he won't take turns."*

Father: *"Those are good, safe things to do if someone won't take turns. I am really proud that you thought of these safer ways of behaving in the future."*

Eric and I continued discussing his behavior and feelings. I also put the bat up for one week, a mild logical consequence for threatening someone with it.

There are many motives for aggressive behavior. A child may try to hurt another person because he is angry and upset, because he wants to get his way, or because he wants to control the other person. As parents, however, we must stop behavior which threatens or hurts others.

A child might also endanger *himself* by disobeying important safety rules or by taking serious risks. For example, a child might ride his tricycle into a busy street, play with matches, or go too near dangerous machinery or equipment.

Perched On The Overpass

Nine-year-old Brandi and her father walked through a large city park. Brandi was being especially difficult to

handle that afternoon and ran ahead of her father, nearly getting lost several times. Father was repeatedly nagging and
shouting, and Brandi was repeatedly "doing her own thing."

As they approached the edge of the park, Brandi darted
ahead and disappeared along the curving sidewalk. Father finally
caught up with her. He found her perched on the edge of a tall
pedestrian overpass, casually looking down on four lanes of traffic moving below her!

Father tried to remain calm, told Brandi to get down slowly, and then he scolded her. He also gave her a nine-minute time-
out under a large tree back in the park. For the rest of their walk,
Brandi had to stay within ten feet of him or she got another *immediate time-out*. Brandi quickly became manageable.

Managing Aggressive And Dangerous Behavior [56,66,78]

A parent has two goals for managing aggressive and dangerous
behavior. The first goal is to immediately stop the misbehavior in order
to protect the safety of the child or others. The second goal is to effectively handle the misbehavior so that it won't occur again in the
future. *In order to meet these two goals, keep in mind the following
basic steps.*

**A. Stop the behavior, deliver a brief scolding, and name the
unacceptable behavior.** Parents sometimes need to immediately step
in and restrain their child when he is behaving aggressively or
dangerously. There is a time for talk and there is a time for action!
Act quickly when the safety of your child or other children is in question.

After stopping the dangerous behavior, deliver a brief, harsh
scolding and name the particular misbehavior. Avoid entering into an
argument or long discussion before sending him to time-out. In a loud,
firm voice, say, *"No! You are never to . . .* (name the aggressive or
dangerous action)!"[66] I emphatically and explicitly told Eric, *"Don't
ever chase anyone with a bat!"*

If the child's actions are serious, I favor giving a couple of swift
swats on the bottom with an open hand for children six and younger.
Swats should be given for misbehavior which is physically dangerous.
If you oppose *ever* spanking your child, as do some parents, then you'll
be skipping this step.

B. Place your child in time-out immediately. When correcting aggressive or dangerous behavior, there is a time to talk and there
is a time to use time-out. Quickly send your child to time-out after stopping his dangerous behavior. Don't skip this important step and do
use a timer!

You may be wondering, *"Will an aggressive child cooperate by
going to time-out?"* The answer is, "YES!" Appendix B tells how to
get a rebellious child to cooperate with the time-out method of discipline.

If both of your children are involved in serious misbehavior and if both are "guilty" to some extent, consider using "time-out for two." Timing-out two children is discussed in Chapter 15.

While your child is in time-out, prepare yourself for the "after time-out" discussion. Mentally rehearse what you are going to say. Think about *why* your child may have behaved dangerously or impulsively.

C. Talk to him about his aggressive or dangerous behavior. After time-out is over, tell your child again what he did that was aggressive or dangerous. Tell him why his behavior was unacceptable. Then ask him to tell you, in his own words, what he did that was dangerous. At this point, you are not asking him to apologize or promise not to do it again. You are merely asking him to *describe* what he did. In the discussion with my son, I said, *"Eric, tell me again. What did you do that was dangerous?"*

After he describes his aggressive or dangerous behavior, ask him to describe several alternative ways of safely behaving in the future. When talking with Eric, I said, *"Tell me, what can you do next time if Cory won't take turns and you get mad? What can you do that is safe?"*

After your child tells you about alternative, safer ways of behaving, give him your praise. Help him discover alternative ways to cope with difficult people and solve problems in the future. Five-year-old Eric told me of several things he might do the next time that Cory refused to take turns— *"I could tell him that I won't play with him if he doesn't take turns . . . . I could tell his mother on him . . . . I could come and tell you that he won't take turns."*

If your child can't seem to think of any alternative, safer ways of behaving, then you should help him to determine some alternatives. If he angrily "clams up" and refuses to talk to you, wait until later to talk, or consider sending him to time-out once more, but only once more. Following this second time-out, again attempt to discuss alternative, safer ways of behaving.

D. Follow through with a mild logical consequence or behavior penalty. Logical consequences and behavior penalties are described in Chapter 5. If your child is small and acts physically aggressive toward the neighborhood bully, he will probably receive a *natural consequence,* such as a black eye or other bruises!

If your son or daughter uses a toy or object when behaving in a dangerous or aggressive way, consider also placing the toy or object in time-out for an extended period of time. Eric lost the use of his bat for one week.

Twelve-year-old Mary enjoyed frightening younger children by riding her bicycle at high speed and then swerving to miss them. She permanently stopped this dangerous behavior after her mother locked up her bicycle for two weeks.

After Brandi's father found her perched on the overpass, he

made her stay within ten feet of him for the rest of their walk that afternoon. This brief *restriction* was a logical consequence for her prior dangerous behavior.

Basic Steps For Handling Aggressive Or Dangerous Behavior— Parents' Check List

Immediate Steps
✔ To Follow:

____ 1. Stop the behavior.

____ 2. Deliver a brief scolding and name the unacceptable behavior.

____ *3. Deliver three swats to his bottom (if he is six or younger).

____ 4. Place him in time-out immediately.

After Time-Out Is Over:

____ 5. Ask him to say what he did that was aggressive or dangerous.

____ 6. Help him describe one or two other ways of behaving safely or nonaggressively in the future. Reward him with your praise after he tells you about these other ways of safely behaving.

___ **7. Follow through with a *mild* logical consequence or behavior penalty. (See Chapter 5)

____ 8. Use reflective listening *if* your child is in the mood to talk. (Chapter 18)

*You may decide that this step is unnecessary, especially if your child's misbehavior isn't serious or if you oppose the use of "swats."
**This step may be unnecessary also, depending on the seriousness of your child's behavior.

E. Use reflective listening if your child is in the mood to talk.
The next chapter shows how to use "reflective listening" so that you
can help your child to express her feelings. Children who understand
their feelings, and know how to express their anger and frustration
with words, have greater control over their aggressive, impulsive
behavior.

More Help For The Aggressive Child[56,59]

Aggressive children maintain a high rate of verbally and
physically aggressive behavior toward family members, other children,
adults (including teachers), and property. These children are quick
to hit, push, kick, bite, spit, tease, torment, have a tantrum, throw
things, and cry. Many children *occasionally* engage in *some* of these
behaviors, but the aggressive child *frequently* engages in *many* of
these behaviors.

Although his aggression is an almost "automatic" response to
stress and frustration, it also has a purpose. *His aggression forces
or coerces others to give him what he wants.* When others resist giving in to his demands or attempt to punish his aggressive behavior,
the aggressive child usually responds by becoming increasingly
belligerent and "out-of-control."

Aggression can lead to grave consequences. Another family
counselor and I worked with nine-year-old Steven and his family.
Steven's parents and the court sought help for him after he impulsively
picked up a pipe and, in a fit of anger, struck and killed another child.
Don't postpone trying to correct a child's aggressive pattern of
behavior.

The aggressive child is usually *noncompliant.* That is, he
doesn't comply with requests from his parents and other adults—he
doesn't mind and obey as well as other children. He "learns that a
temper tantrum is an effective means of training parents to stop asking him to do things he doesn't want to do."[56]

It's difficult to help the aggressive child—or even like him. He
can keep a family or an entire classroom in angry turmoil. The aggressive child is usually a boy, but girls can also develop this pattern
of behavior. Parents and teachers who try to help the aggressive child
often have a lot of difficulty dealing with their own feelings of anger
and frustration toward the child.

Many parents with an angry, out-of-control child secretly hope
that a hidden inner cause for their child's aggressive behavior can
be found. They also want to believe that they can *send* their child to
a professional who will discover an "inner problem" and fix their child's
personality and behavior by using a new, powerful method of therapy.
Parents at the other extreme feel helpless and believe that nothing
can be done to help their son or daughter.

The truth is that the aggressive child can be helped and sometimes dramatically changed. However, helping the aggressive child requires much from parents. It requires hard work, patience, "follow-through," caring and the systematic application of the *behavioral methods* described in this book. Professional help is often necessary as well. Chapter 22 discusses when and how to get professional help.

PROBLEMS PARENTS FACE

"All I did was ask her to take out the trash. I guess that she doesn't want to do it!"

The aggressive child often has temper tantrums when told to do things that she doesn't want to do.

When the aggressive child *acts* aggressively and dangerously toward others, consistently follow the "Basic Steps For Handling Aggressive Or Dangerous Behavior" described earlier. Every time that he makes *verbal threats,* simply use a time-out or another method of mild punishment such as a logical counsequence or behavior penalty.

Be sure to reward the aggressive child with attention and praise when he behaves nonaggressively and when he minds. Also, consider beginning a point-reward program to help him improve his behavior, as described in Chapter 14. Allow him to earn points for each half-day that is free of aggressive behavior. After earning points, he trades them for material and activity rewards.

Many children who are aggressive at home are also aggressive at school. Coordinate your efforts to reduce your child's aggressive behavior with the efforts of his teacher. Study Chapter 19 to learn how to work effectively with your child's teacher. Reducing aggression requires a coordinated "attack"!

I recommend reading a short book called *Families*[56] by Gerald Patterson. You will learn more applications of behavioral methods to help aggressive and noncompliant children.

Children often increase aggressive behavior by being exposed to "models" who act verbally or physically aggressive. As mentioned in earlier chapters, be sure that you and your spouse are good models. Also help your child to avoid excessive exposure to aggressive peers and television programs.

Main Points To Remember:

1. Use the "Basic Steps For Handling Aggressive or Dangerous Behavior" whenever you see that behavior occur.
2. You can help the *aggressive child* to improve his pattern of behavior by using the methods of child management described in *SOS!*

Chapter 18

Helping Your Child To Express Feelings

"They said that you couldn't play with them because you are a girl? . . . I can see why you feel hurt and angry. . . ."

"No Girls Allowed!"

Relaxing in his easy chair, father jumped when ten-year-old Stacy slammed the front door and entered the room. Wearing a baseball cap, glove, and an angry scowl, she said, *"Next time I am going to use my bat on those boys!"*

Father: *"What happened, Stacy? Tell me about it."*

Stacy: *"I went out to play ball and those mean boys wouldn't let me play!"*

Father: *"They wouldn't let you play?"*

Stacy: *"No! They said, 'No girls allowed' and then they all laughed at me!"*

Father: *"They said that you couldn't play with them because you are a girl? . . . I can see why you feel hurt and angry . . . ."*

Stacy: *"Yes, they made me mad! And they hurt my feelings, too. I thought that they were my friends."*

Father gave Stacy emotional support by being concerned, listening, and reflecting her feelings. He helped her to realize that she was feeling more than just anger. She was also feeling hurt and rejected.

We like to protect our children from disappointments, frustrations, and conflicts with other people. However, we can't constantly keep them under our "protective wing." What we *can do* is help them to understand and cope with their feelings from unpleasant experiences. By using *reflective listening,* we encourage our children to express and share feelings with us. *Reflective listening is briefly summarizing and restating to your child both her feelings and the situation causing those feelings.* *

By sharing unpleasant feelings with you, your child will be less hurt or burdened by them. She'll also gain increased control over her emotions and behavior, and will make better choices in meeting the challenges of daily living. Communication with your child will improve and you'll have a closer relationship.

How early should parents begin reflective listening? Three-year-olds aren't too young to benefit if parents are brief and use simple words. Boys need help in expressing feelings as much as girls. Boys and girls who are "in touch with their own feelings" become better adjusted men and women.

Basic Skills Of Reflective Listening[18,23,33]

Use the communication skill of reflective listening to help your child to learn to express her feelings. *Follow five guidelines when your child begins to share her feelings with you:*

1. Accept and respect all of your child's feelings. Do this by listening quietly and attentively and being nonjudgmental. Of course you needn't accept all of her *actions or behaviors,* just her feelings. She can tell you how angry she is at her brother, but she isn't permitted to show aggression by teasing or hitting him.

2. Show her that you are listening to what she says.[23] Your close attention rewards her for expressing her ideas and feelings to you. Stop what you are doing, turn toward her, maintain eye contact,

---

*Reflective listening is also called "active listening."

and listen carefully. Also, show her your attention by nodding your head and by an occasional, *"Um hum . . . yes . . . Mmm . . ."*

3. Tell your child what you hear her saying and what you think she is feeling. Occasionally summarize, restate, or rephrase the core of what she tells you—both her *feelings* and the *situation* which caused her feelings. It's not enough to only listen and understand. You must also *reflect back to her, with words, what she is saying, thinking, and feeling.* This is *reflective listening*—a skill which takes practice. Try not to repeat your daughter's *exact words.* Use *similar words* that capture the same meaning and feeling. Say to your disappointed three-year-old, *"You feel bad* (the feeling) *because you couldn't go to the store with Daddy this time* (the situation)."

Your child may say things which you find terribly upsetting or threatening. For example, she may say, *"No one at school likes me!"* Brace yourself and don't be swept away by a flood of concern or guilt as you listen and reflect what she says. Be a helpful parent and encourage her to express *whatever* she feels. She needs your help. By being an effective sounding board and mirror for your child, you are helping her to cope with her feelings and to make better choices and plans for herself.

Children often exaggerate both their negative feelings and the distasteful situation behind those feelings. Help your child understand and clarify her feelings and her description of the situation by using reflective listening. However, *don't* tell her that she is exaggerating because this will make her less willing to share other feelings with you.

4. Give her feelings a name. After listening carefully to what she says and watching her facial expressions, make an "educated guess" and tentatively label her feelings. For example, say to your nine-year-old, *"You seem to be feeling disappointed* (a feeling) *or perhaps a little resentful* (another feeling) *because of the way your teacher treated you* (the situation)." If you are incorrect with your first guess, then try again. Be respectful, calm, and maintain a slow pace in what you say. Encourage her to tell you if your guess is wrong and to help you correct your guess.

The list "Names For Unpleasant Feelings" gives labels for common negative feelings that confront children and adults. If your child is young, be sure to use simple words when you label her feelings.

5. Offer advice, suggestions, reassurance, or alternative ways of looking at things, only AFTER you help your child to examine how she feels. Advice, suggestions, and reassurance, if given first, will hamper your child's effort to express her feelings.

How do you begin learning the skill of reflective listening? The technique for reflecting positive feelings is the same as for reflecting negative feelings. Most parents find it easier and more pleasant to practice the skill of reflective listening by beginning with their child's positive feelings.

Names For Unpleasant Feelings

angry, mad   *unhappy, miserable*
resentful, want to get even   *messed over, unfair*
irritable, grumpy   *unloved, neglected*
scared, afraid   *discouraged*
disappointed, let down   *embarrassed*
lonely, left out   *hurt*
without a friend, rejected   *tired*
worthless, no good   *bored*
stupid, dumb   *confused*
upset, tense   *frustrated*
worried, anxious   *inferior*
insecure

The next time that your child tells you something and seems to have positive feelings (such as feeling excited, relieved, eager, proud, or happy) reflect these feelings. Also, reflect her description of the situation or event which caused the feelings. For example, say, *"You seem to feel relieved* (the feeling) *because your piano recital was cancelled* (the situation)." Or say, *"Getting invited to Mike's party,* (the situation) *has sure made you feel excited and happy* (the feeling)." *Practice* the skill of reflective listening in order to learn it.

"I Feel Like I Don't Have A Friend Anymore"

When my oldest son, Eric, was four, I found him crying by our swing set in the back yard. Tears were streaming down through the dirt covering his face. Sobbing, he said, *"I hate Kenneth! He threw dirt in my face!"* I tried to reflect his feelings by saying, *"You're mad at Kenneth for throwing dirt and also he hurt your feelings."* He replied, *"Yes, I feel like I don't have a friend anymore!"*

We walked to the house and I helped wash off the dirt. More important, I helped him cope with an insult from a friend by simply reflecting his feelings of anger and hurt. Later that afternoon, I watched Eric and Kenneth happily playing together.

Reflective Listening And Problems Parents Face

Several problems may arise when your child expresses feelings to you. You can manage each of these problems!

Problem A—Your child expresses unpleasant feelings toward you. She may say, *"You won't let me go to the movies Friday night and I'm mad at you!"* Allow her to express negative feelings toward you, but don't permit her to verbally "abuse" you. Don't allow her to call you names, swear at you, threaten or have a screaming tantrum. Tell her that she may express her feelings, but that you won't

tolerate verbal abuse. If she continues with name calling or screaming, consider leaving the room or using mild punishment.

Children must learn to express their feelings without being aggressive, obnoxious, and verbally abusive. Also, when *you* express
your feelings toward your child, be sure that you "follow the rules"
too, and don't verbally abuse him or her. Be a good model!

**Problem B—You help your child to talk about her feelings.
However, she continues feeling miserable or voices irrational
plans.** Even after you have listened carefully, given her useful suggestions, and mentioned the possible consequences of her actions,
twelve-year-old Laura may still be unreasonable. She may walk away
saying, *"My English teacher is mean and unfair and I hate her! But
I'm going to show her. She'll be sorry. I'm going to keep whispering
in class and I'm going to hand my report in late!"* Often we can't directly
change our child's irrational feelings and plans. Laura may have to
learn to improve her behavior through natural consequences—the
"School of Hard Knocks." That is, she may continue having to stay
late after school for whispering in class and she may get an "F" on
that late report.

**Problem C—Your child is critical of your attempts at reflec-
tive listening.** Consider the following discussion between mother and
ten-year-old Bradley.

> Bradley: *"I'm mad at Chad's parents. They won't let him do
> anything. They're always afraid he'll get hurt. They treat
> him like a baby."*
>
> Mother: *"You are saying that you are annoyed at his parents
> because they baby him?"*
>
> Bradley: *"That's what I said! There you go again, repeating what
> I say!"*
>
> Mother: *"Well, Bradley, I am interested in your thoughts about
> Chad and his parents."*
>
> Bradley: *"O.K. One way that they baby him is not letting him go
> with me to . . . ."*

If your child remarks on your reflective listening, simply "keep
your cool" and tell him that you are concerned about his feelings and
thoughts. Don't let your child's reactions toward your reflective listening skills keep you from being a helpful parent.*

---

*Read *The Parents Handbook: STEP,*[18] an interesting book by Don
Dinkmeyer and Gary McKay, which describes more methods for helping
children to express feelings.

Main Points To Remember:

1. *Reflective listening* is summarizing and restating to your child, both his feelings and the situation causing those feelings.
2. Use reflective listening to actively help your child understand and cope with his feelings.
3. Reflective listening also helps children gain increased *control* over their emotions and behavior.

Chapter 19

More Problem Behaviors— Questions And Solutions

"Always in motion! Is this normal for a six-year-old?"

In this chapter, we'll look at a variety of common childhood problems such as *hyperactivity, specific learning disability, bedwetting, daytime enuresis, resisting chores, and bedtime problems.* You'll learn more methods and skills for helping your child, including *"racing the timer,"* grounding, and the *"resting chair."* Also, you'll discover additional ways of using *point-rewards.* Let's look at questions parents frequently ask.

Q: *"My six-year-old son, Jeremy, is very active, always in motion, and doesn't pay attention when I tell him things. His first grade teacher says that he is 'hyperactive.' How can I tell if Jeremy is hyperactive and, if so, what can I do to help him?"*

A: A hyperactive child is persistently overactive, inattentive, and impulsive when compared with other children of the same age. Many hyperactive children experience school learning problems, have difficulty in getting along with peers, and are aggressive. Hyperactivity is about ten times more common in boys than in girls.[3,7] Parents and teachers usually report feeling frustrated and worn-out as they try to keep up with hyperactive children.

PROBLEMS PSYCHOLOGISTS FACE—
WHEN TESTING *HYPERACTIVE* CHILDREN

*"Why is he messing up my things? Who is in charge
here anyway?"*

To determine if Jeremy is hyperactive, have him examined by a pediatrician and also evaluated by a psychologist. The psychologist probably will want to talk with Jeremy's teacher as well. Be consistent in applying the methods of child management described in this book. It's particularly important to give him lots of praise for completing an activity or chore. Your pediatrician and psychologist will give you additional recommendations if they feel that Jeremy needs special help.

Q: *"My six-year-old daughter dawdles when straightening her room, dressing for school, and going to bed. Is there any way that I can help her to speed up?"*

A: To speed up your daughter's slow behavior, try an effective method called "racing the timer."[44] Set a kitchen timer for a short period of time and reward her if she completes a task before the timer rings. For example, the next time that you announce it's bedtime, set a timer for 30 or 40 minutes. Tell her that she gets a bedtime story and a point on the point-reward calendar if she beats the timer. To beat the timer, she must finish her bedtime snack, put on her pajamas, brush her teeth, and be in bed when the timer rings.

Don't nag her to hurry and don't scold her if she loses the race. However, when she beats the timer, give her praise, a point on the calendar, and a bedtime story!

Q: *"Are there more ways that timers may be used to help children?"*

A: There are at least five ways that timers can help improve behavior.[42] Parents can *time-out one child, two or more children, or toys* that are involved in misbehavior. A timer can *help children take turns* when they want to play with the same toy, such as a video game. Also, as discussed previously, children can *"race the timer"* in order to speed up slow behavior. Timers are "parent savers" because they are easy to use, effective in changing behavior, and save "wear and tear" on parents. Timers are also "child savers" because they save children from listening to nagging and lecturing by parents.[52]

Q: *"Occasionally, our twelve-year-old daughter gets in a bad mood, is grumpy, grouchy, complains about everything, criticizes her younger sister, and says annoying things to the rest of the family. Do you believe in sending a child to her room for this unpleasant behavior?"*

A: Yes, but first try reflective listening to determine what may be bothering her. I've described the skill of reflective listening in Chapter 18. Perhaps nothing specific is troubling your daughter; being grouchy with her family may be a "bad habit." Tell her that you understand that she feels "grumpy." She has a right to her feelings, but she shouldn't subject the family to abusive behavior. *Don't call it time-out, but send her to her room.* Tell her that she may come out when she can stop grumbling, complaining, and criticizing her sister. Don't tell her how long to stay in her room; *she* decides when to come out. Fatigue sometimes causes grumpiness. If your daughter is grouchy because she is tired, then she might decide to take a short nap before rejoining the family.

Q: *"My seven- and ten-year-old children avoid helping my husband and me when we wash the car, rake leaves, or do dishes. They often say that they feel sick or tired or that they don't want to help. Are there any more methods which encouarage children to help parents with work?"*

A: A "resting chair" encourages children to help parents with chores! This is the plan. Everyone who begins a chore works until it is completed—all the leaves are raked. If someone claims to feel sick or too tired to help the family, then that person must sit on the resting chair. The resting chair doesn't have to be an actual chair. If you are working outdoors, a spot under a particular tree will do fine. Be sure that the place is dull, boring, and free of interesting objects, but near another family member who *is* working. The person who is working serves as a good "model" for the child who is resting!

A truly tired child—or adult—welcomes the opportunity to rest. However, children who pretend to be tired soon get bored merely sitting in the resting chair and watching others. Most children will decide to leave the resting chair and help others with chores because they prefer some kind of activity to inactivity. Don't scold your child for sitting on the resting chair rather than working. Be sure that he doesn't get attention, play with toys, or leave the chair except to help others finish the job. A *resting chair* is boring, and boredom helps motivate children to work! After your children help with chores be sure to tell them that you appreciate their hard work.

Q: *"My nine-year-old son, Brandon, still wets the bed at night. I've heard that an alarm for bedwetting can help children to have dry nights. Could such an alarm help my son?"*

A: Yes! Bedwetting alarms can help children six and older to attain dry nights. Most children stop nighttime enuresis—wetting the bed—by the age of five or six. If they don't, they might need special help from their parents.

First, take Brandon to your pediatrician to be sure that a medical problem isn't causing his bedwetting. Next, begin a special program to help Brandon. Follow these steps:

1. Use a "point-reward calendar for improving one behavior," as described in Chapter 14. The desired target behavior is dry nights, and Brandon should get a point for each night that he doesn't wet the bed. When he accumulates enough points, he selects a reward from a "menu of rewards."

Also, give him a lot of praise for each dry night. Never

scold or shame him for wetting the bed! Undoubtedly, he *already* feels embarrassed or humiliated because of his problem.

2. *Whenever Brandon discovers that he wet the bed, he is to immediately shower or bathe and then place his wet sheets in the washer.* This is a mild logical consequence for wetting his bed. Younger children need help from a parent in stripping a bed and drawing bath water. Steps one and two are often sufficient to help many children to completely stop wetting the bed within one or two months. However, if Brandon persists in bedwetting, continue with these two steps and begin step three.

3. *Order a bedwetting alarm* from a mail-order catalog store such as Sears. The child sleeps on a special pad which senses moisture and activates a battery powered alarm. Since it takes only two seconds for the alarm to sound, Brandon will get *instant feedback* that he wet the bed. *He will learn to correct his bedwetting by "conditioning."* He may need to use the alarm for a couple of months before he overcomes the problem.

An alarm is extremely effective in helping children and adolescents to stop wetting the bed.[71] However, if you purchase an alarm, also continue following steps one and two. After attaining dry nights, your child may *return* to bedwetting. Don't despair! Simply follow the steps again. Most children don't return to bedwetting after a second time through the program.

If you correctly follow all three steps and your son or daughter persists in bedwetting, consider reading *A Parent's Guide To Bedwetting Control* by Nathan Azrin and Victoria Besalel.[4] Also, you may wish to consult your pediatrician, a psychologist, or another behavioral specialist for additional help.

Q: *"What help do you recommend for children who wet on themselves during the day, after they become toilet trained?"*

A: A child who is five or older and toilet trained may slip back into occasional *daytime* enuresis. Try the following program:

Each day that your child is dry, give her three points on the point-reward calendar. If her problem is more frequent than once a day, then divide the day into morning, afternoon, and evening. Give her a point for each part of the day that she is accident free. She can earn up to three points a day!

Encourage her to exchange her points for an item on the *reward menu* as soon as she earns enough points. Also, at the end of each day compliment her if she hasn't had any accidents that day.

Never scold her for having an accident. Instead, have her immediately bathe, put on fresh clothes, and rinse out the soiled clothes herself.

Q: *"My neighbors tell me that they restrict or 'ground' their thirteen-year-old son for two or three weeks when he breaks rules. What is grounding, and do you recommend it as a method of discipline? I am thinking about using it with my teenage daughter."*

A: "Grounding" is briefly restricting a child or adolescent to her home as a consequence for bad behavior. She isn't permitted to visit friends or to go places without her parents as she normally does. When used correctly, *grounding can help preadolescents and teenagers to improve their behavior.*

If you use grounding, be sure that you follow two rules.[36] *Tell your child in advance what misbehavior will cause grounding.* Also, *always keep the duration of grounding short*—usually not more than a weekend or one week. Grounding a teenager for a period of two or three weeks is overly severe and is not an effective method for improving behavior.

Q: *"My nine-year-old daughter, April, earns poor marks in school. Her teacher says that she may have a 'specific learning disability.' What is a 'specific learning disability' and what should I do next in order to help my daughter?"*

A: A specific learning disability means that a child's skill in reading, writing, or arithmetic is significantly below her age and intellectual capacity.[3] Your daughter should be evaluated by a pediatrician and an eye doctor. It's also essential that a psychologist talk to you and your daughter and obtain measures of her intellectual capacity and educational skills. Be sure to follow the recommendations of the pediatrician and psychologist. A book by Osmon, described in Chapter 21, gives parents suggestions for helping children with learning disabilities.[55]

Main Points To Remember:
1. This chapter gives parents recommendations for common childhood problems such as hyperactivity, going to bed on time, resisting chores, bedwetting, daytime enuresis, and specific learning disability.
2. Effective methods described in this chapter for helping children improve their behavior are racing the timer, sending a child to her room (not to time-out), the resting chair, grounding, and point-rewards.
3. Contact a pediatrician, psychologist or family counselor for more help if the child management methods that you're using aren't effective in helping your child.

Section Four

MORE RESOURCES FOR HELPING YOUR CHILD

You're not alone in the challenges of being a parent and assisting your son or daughter. Read this section and learn about various resources for parents.

Teachers spend many hours each week helping children. The next chapter tells how to work more effectively with your child's teacher. You'll also learn about joining parent education classes and about additional parenting books. The last chapter tells when and how to get professional help for your child or family.

Let's look at resources for parents!

Chapter 20

Teachers And Parents As Partners

PROBLEMS TEACHERS FACE

No one said that handling children is *easy*.

In this chapter, you'll learn how to help improve your child's classroom work and personal adjustment by working effectively with his teacher. You'll also learn about methods which teachers use to manage children.

Working With Your Child's Teacher

Build a positive relationship with your child's teacher and demonstrate an interest in your child's school experiences by visiting the classroom. Quickly respond to notes from the teacher and school. Be the first to sign up to bring snacks and drinks for your son or daughter's class. Your child will appreciate the additional attention and interest in her classroom.

If you have time, consider volunteering to help the teacher. After first discussing it with your son or daughter, donate some of your time to your child's class. You might rearrange bulletin boards, organize bookshelves or complete records.

Talk to your child about school. Children often bring their papers and completed projects home. Spend some time looking at your child's work. The best way for you to increase his good work is to reward it with attention and praise. Some parents even post their child's school papers on the refrigerator door for the whole family to admire!

Don't say negative things about the teacher in your child's presence. You want your child to respect the teacher. Also, remember that children frequently repeat things to their teacher that they hear at home!

Plan ahead if you want a productive parent-teacher conference. *A parent-teacher conference is a face-to-face meeting between you and your child's teacher.* As partners, you plan the best way to meet your child's educational and personal needs. What do you talk about at a conference? You might discuss your child's study habits, need for remedial work, or how to help her get along better with other children.

Most schools contact parents and schedule at least one or two conferences a year. However, you have the right to ask for additional conferences if your child needs special help. Don't be passive and wait for the teacher to contact you if your child is having difficulties. Don't assume if you hear nothing from the teacher that everything is fine, especially if your child has had school problems in the past.

Consider the following guidelines when contacting your child's teacher for a conference.[12]

1. Ask the teacher, at least a day in advance, to *schedule a time* to discuss your child's progress and adjustment. Don't just "drop in" on the teacher and expect to have a productive conference. To talk to the teacher about a problem or to schedule a conference, call the school and ask that the teacher return your call.

2. Make a list of things that you want to tell the teacher about your child and make a list of questions that you have about your child's progress. Ask about your child's strongest and weakest subject areas and about any adjustment or behavior problems. If your spouse can't attend the conference, ask him or her for ideas when preparing your list.

3. Don't bring your child to the conference unless the teacher specifically requests that you bring her. Also, leave her brothers and sisters at home so that you and the teacher can devote full attention to discussing your child.

4. During the conference, decide on *specific plans* to help your child. Ask the teacher for suggestions and recommendations and honestly give these ideas a try. Agree on what the teacher is to do at school and what you are to do at home to help your child. Take notes concerning these future plans. Encourage the teacher to contact you if your child begins having problems at school.

5. Be pleasant and nurture a positive working partnership between you and your child's teacher. Tell the teacher that you appreciate the help that he or she is giving your child. If you feel that the teacher is doing a good job, let the teacher know it. Reward the teacher's "good behavior"!

Avoid getting upset and angry at the teacher and the school. Look for solutions to your child's problems, but *avoid making the teacher feel responsible for those problems.* Recognize that the teacher has at least 20 other children in the classroom. Understand the goals that the teacher and the school have for *all* children.

6. Following your meeting with the teacher, share the results of the conference with your spouse and ask for help in following through with any suggestions and recommendations. After the conference, tell your child about his strengths, problem areas needing improvement, and any plan of action decided upon by you and the teacher.

7. Keep in close touch with your child's teacher. Don't be afraid to ask for additional conferences. Teachers enjoy working with concerned parents who are strongly interested in their children. Teachers shouldn't mind additional conferences as long as you aren't blaming them for your child's problems.

If you child's teacher agrees, use a *parent-teacher-child record form* to improve your child's school work or behavior problems. Each day, the child takes the record form between home and school. The teacher indicates on the form whether or not a particular target behavior has occurred at school. When the child takes the record home, the parent can see if the target behavior occurred that day. The child then gains or loses a privilege at home that same afternoon or evening.

For example, seven-year-old John completed his morning seatwork only 62 percent of the time during a two-week period. He had the ability to do better, but he spent his time daydreaming and bothering children sitting near him. His teacher asked him and his parents to attend a joint conference where it was agreed to use the record form to help him.

Each day that John completed all of his morning seatwork, he earned the privilege of watching television at home between 3:00 p.m. and 5:00 p.m. that afternoon. If he failed to complete his seatwork or if he forgot the record form, then he couldn't watch television during those hours. John improved and instead of completing his seatwork only 62 percent of the time, he completed it 94 percent of the time! See the "Parent-Teacher-Child Record Form" used to help John.

Parent-Teacher-Child Record Form—
Record Of John's Target Behavior

Record of _____John's_____ Target Behavior
(child's name)

Week of: ___May 7th to 11th___

	M	T	W	T	F
Target behavior: _All morning_ seatwork completed; yes or no (teacher records each day)	No	No	Yes	Yes	Yes
Teacher's initials: (teacher signs each day)	CC	CC	CC	CC	CC
Child's initials: (child signs each day)	jb	jb	jb	jb	jb
Parent's initials: (parent signs each evening)	MB	MB	MB	MB	MB

Plan: _If John completes all morning seatwork, he gets_
to watch television at home between 3:00 p.m. and 5:00 p.m.
If seatwork is not completed or if John fails to bring this form
home, then no television between 3:00 p.m. and 5:00 p.m.

Each day that John completes his seatwork at school, he gets the privilege of watching television at home that afternoon. For a copy of a "Parent-Teacher-Child Record Form" see the tear-out sheets at the end of this book.

Some record forms state that a privilege will be lost *if* a particular *undesired* target behavior such as fighting or teasing other children *occurs.* A record form provides the child, teacher, and parent with daily feedback regarding the progress of the target behavior. The record keeps everyone *involved and coordinated* in trying to improve the problem behavior. Since the record form requires extra time from the teacher, tell her that you appreciate her additional help.

When your child is upset about other children, the teacher, or classwork, use *reflective listening* to help him to express his feelings and thoughts. Reflective listening skills are discussed in the preceding chapter.

If your child has continuing difficulty with her school work, you might consider obtaining a psychological evaluation of her educational skills, intellectual abilities, and level of motivation. The school might provide this evaluation. If not, you'll need to contact a psychologist yourself. (See Chapter 22 which tells when and how to get professional help.)

Teachers Managing Behavior

Read this section if you are interested in methods teachers may use in managing children.

PROBLEMS TEACHERS FACE

"My little Scott is a BITER. He bites EVERYONE. I hope that you can do something with him!"

Teachers must deal with a wide range of behavior problems.

Teachers state that the most difficult and stressful part of their job is "managing behavior." Unfortunately, few colleges and universities require a special course which teaches specific methods and techniques of classroom discipline and behavior management.*

Nearly all of the behavior management methods described in SOS! Help For Parents are used by teachers in the classroom. Some teachers effectively use a wide variety of discipline methods. Other teachers are less effective, use a narrower range of methods, and misuse some methods.

Effective teachers know that rewarding good behavior is the best way to improve behavior. They use *activity and material rewards* as well as *social rewards* such as praise and attention.

"Three Cheers For The Token Jar!"

Mrs. Pierce wanted an effective way to help her second graders to improve their problem behavior. Alicia was often out of her seat, roaming about the classroom. Robert couldn't see the chalkboard or his seatwork unless he wore his glasses. However, he usually left them at home. Adam couldn't keep his hands to himself and he often pushed and hit others. Lori rarely completed her seatwork and spent most of her time daydreaming or trying to talk to other children.

One morning Mrs. Pierce brought some poker chips and a clear plastic jar to school. The jar had a black line on it. Holding the jar and poker chips up high for her class to see, she announced, *"Each of you may earn tokens and put them in the token jar. You can earn tokens by behaving in ways that help you or help our class. When the tokens come up to this black line, you all get to share a treat!"*

Alicia earned tokens by staying in her seat. When he remembered to wear his glasses to school, Robert got a token for the jar. The teacher gave Adam a token when he went one hour without hitting or pushing. *The teacher "caught" other children being good and rewarded them with tokens too.* When earning a token, the children also received approving smiles from their classmates.

The students were excited Friday afternoon because the tokens were almost touching the black line. All the students cheered when Alicia earned two tokens for turning in her seatwork. When she dropped her tokens in the jar, the accummulated tokens came up to the black line. Mrs. Pierce then gave each child a small candy bar. She also announced that the class could earn another reward—extra recess time for everyone—by filling the jar again.

Since all children may earn tokens and all share in the eventual reward, the children give each other a lot of

---

*A helpful book on managing behavior, written especially for teachers, is *Teaching/Discipline: A Positive Approach For Educational Development* by Charles Madsen and Clifford Madsen.[46]

encouragement for demonstrating positive behavior. *A token jar is an effective way to increase a variety of desirable behaviors without any record keeping.*

Teachers also use *scolding and disapproval* as well as *active ignoring* to reduce problem behavior. *Behavior penalty, natural consequences,* and *logical consequences,* described in Chapter 5, are other effective discipline methods.

Trading A Dry Shirt For A Wet One

Shane splashed water in the school rest room and drenched Joshua's shirt! Shane also laughed and poked fun at Joshua and his wet shirt.

When both boys returned to their fourth grade classroom, the teacher made them trade shirts. Shane got to "wear" the problem he caused—the wet shirt! To deal with the problem behavior, the teacher used a *logical consequence*—Shane's punishment fit his crime!

Some preschool and elementary teachers effectively use time-out for handling persistent problem behavior.* Your child may refer to the "quiet chair," the "lonesome chair," or simply the "chair" when telling you about time-out.

"Todd Put Patti In Time-Out Today!"

Although only two and a half years old, my son Todd was "experienced" in the time-out method. My wife and I used time-out to manage his misbehavior at home, and his day-care center also employed time-out.

Late one afternoon when my wife picked up Todd, she asked one of the day-care workers how Todd's day had gone. The worker responded, *"Guess what happened! Todd put Patti in time-out today!"* She further explained, *"I came into the playroom and found Patti, who is also two, quietly sitting on the time-out chair with Todd standing nearby. I asked what happened. Todd said that he made Patti get on the chair because she was 'bad' and threw blocks!"*

At the young age of two, Todd had already become an "old hand" with the time-out method!

Three versions of time-out may be used to help improve the behavior of school children.[1,50]

---

*If you are a teacher and want a brief description of time-out to give to parents, see the sheet "Information For Parents," included at the end of this book.

"NON-EXCLUSION" TIME-OUT

"All I did was HIT Jonathan once!"

1. Non-exclusion time-out. The child isn't excluded from the group. She is seated alone at a particular place or on a special chair. She can still observe group activities, but she can't participate. Other children are told not to tease or talk to a child who is in time-out. If they do, then they run the risk of being sent to time-out also!

"ISOLATION" TIME-OUT

*"I wish I had a book to look at or something
to play with!"*

2. Isolation time-out. If your child is in isolation time-out, he is briefly isolated from the group and all activities. He can't see or talk to the others. A good place for isolation time-out is on a large chair placed behind a file cabinet, screen, or bookcase. Isolation time-out frequently is more effective than non-exclusion time-out in changing behavior. Since two children often misbehave at the same time, two separate time-out places are needed in a classroom.

3. Separate room time-out. The child is removed from other children and interesting activities and is *briefly placed in a separate room.* She isn't required to sit any particular place and is free to move about the room. The room should be boring, well-lighted, safe, and not scary. Separate room time-out shouldn't be used with preschoolers since, for safety's sake, they should always be monitored by adults.

Main Points To Remember:
1. Keep in close touch with the teacher to improve your child's behavior at school.
2. Demonstrate an interest in your child's school experiences by visiting the classroom and by talking to him about school.
3. The behavior management methods described in *SOS!* are used by *teachers* as well as parents.

Chapter 21

Useful Classes And Books For Parents

"Wow! I'm going to try this idea!"

You'll want to continue learning additional parenting skills. This chapter tells how to join a parent education class or organize a parent study group. We'll also look at additional books which teach more parenting skills.

Joining Parent Education Classes—What To Expect

Parent education classes are offered in most communities. The classes provide increased knowledge and skills in child management. Usually six to twelve parents and a group leader meet for five to ten sessions, with each session lasting one or two hours.

Leaders of parent education classes teach by using tapes or films and by directing the group discussion. The group members learn principles of behavior and parenting strategies which are important in assisting *all* children, not just children with emotional or behavioral problems. These classes are not therapy sessions and the group

159

leader won't attempt to diagnose or treat the problems of individual children.

Some parents who participate in parent education classes may have children who are experiencing significant emotional or behavioral problems. However, parent education classes usually deal with the normal challenges of rearing children faced by most parents.

Class leaders may follow the behavioral approach or they may use another orientation such as *P.E.T.*[33] or *STEP.*[18] You'll find that *behavioral* parent education classes are particularly consistent with *SOS!*

How do you find out about parent education classes in your community? These classes may be offered at child guidance clinics, adult education centers, mental health clinics, schools, churches, synagogues, community centers, and child development and psychology departments of universities. You may need to call several of these organizations in order to learn about the next classes scheduled in your community.

Forming Parent Study Groups

Some parents form small informal study groups and discuss common problems of rearing children.[49] Discussions often center around a particular topic or child management book such as *SOS! Help For Parents.* Parents whose children are about the same age form a group. They have weekly meetings at each other's homes or at some place in the community. Toddlers can play while parents talk. However, normally it's more relaxing for parents to meet while their children are at preschool or elementary school.

To begin a parent study group, all you need are three or four parents who are interested in meeting together. You might consider organizing such a group yourself! In order for meetings to continue, a group member should agree to act as a coordinator or discussion leader for each succeeding meeting. Don't let one parent dominate the group discussion. Avoid discussing a son or daughter in front of that child or in the presence of other children.

Other Books Written For Parents

These books may be ordered from your local bookstore or the publisher.

Parenting Books *With* A Behavioral Approach

Allen, J. (1984). *What Do I Do When?* San Luis Obispo, Calif.: Impact Publishers.
The author presents methods for managing over 50 common child-rearing problems.

Eimers, R. & Aitchison, R. (1977). *Effective Parents/Responsible Children.* New York: McGraw-Hill Book Co.
The authors present specific skills for childrearing. Separate sections tell how parents can help slow learners, withdrawn children, and hyperactive children.

Patterson, G. (1975). *Families: Applications of Social Learning to Family Life.* Champaign, Ill.: Research Press.
Basic principles of behavior are discussed. The author presents ways parents can help children who have a variety of problems. This parenting book is often recommended by behavioral family therapists.

Patterson, G. (in press). *Parents and Adolescents Living Together.* Eugene, Oregon: Castalia Publishing Co.
The author presents effective methods that parents of teenagers can employ in order to improve family life.

Parenting Books *Without* A Behavioral Approach

Dinkmeyer, D. & McKay, G. (1976). *The Parent's Handbook: Systematic Training for Effective Parenting.* Circle Pines, Minn.: American Guidance Service.
This cartoon illustrated book presents the childrearing principles of the late Rudolf Dreikurs. The book emphasizes the use of natural and logical consequences; utilizes a family council approach to solving problems; and teaches parents how to help their children to express feelings. It is frequently used in parent education classes. A Spanish edition is available.

Dinkmeyer, D. & McKay, G. (1983). *The Parent's Guide: STEP/Teen: Systematic Training for Effective Parenting of Teens.* Circle Pines, Minn.: American Guidance Service.
The orientation of this illustrated book is the same as the above book by Drs. Dinkmeyer and McKay. However, the book is for parents of teenagers.

Dreikurs, R. & Soltz, V. (1964). *Children: The Challenge.* New York: Hawthorne.
The orientation of this book is similar to the orientation of the books by Drs. Dinkmeyer and McKay described above.

Faber, A. & Mazlish, E. (1980). *How To Talk So Kids Will Listen & Listen So Kids Will Talk.* New York: Avon.
This illustrated book teaches effective communication skills to parents. The authors' orientation toward childrearing is influenced by the psychologist Haim Ginott, whose books are also listed below.

Ginott, H. (1965). *Between Parent and Child.* New York: Avon.
The author tells parents how to communicate with children and how to build mutual respect between parent and child.

Ginnott, H. (1971). *Between Parent and Teenager.* New York: Avon.
This book has the same orientation as the above book, but is intended for parents of teenagers.

Gordon, T. (1970). *P.E.T.: Parent Effectiveness Training.* New York: Plume.
This approach to childrearing stresses communication skills for parents.

Osmon, B. (1979). *Learning Disabilities: A Family Affair.* New York: Random House.
This book gives realistic suggestions for helping children who are of normal intelligence but who have a learning disability.

Main Points To Remember:
1. Consider taking a *parent education class.*
2. Think about organizing a *parent study group.*
3. Learn additional parenting skills by reading one of the previously mentioned books.

Chapter 22

When And How To Get Professional Help

Office of:
DR. B. F. SKINNER
Psychologist

RECEPTIONIST

JOHN ROBB

"Can family counseling help us with our little Tiffany?"

Raising children from infancy through adolescence is a long and sometimes difficult journey. Problems can arise and interfere with your family's well-being and happiness. If difficulties persist in spite of your efforts to resolve them, avoid giving in to hopelessness, guilt, depression, or anger. Contact a counselor or therapist for professional help. Consider the following questions and suggestions when thinking about counseling for your child or family.

Q: *"When should I get professional help for my child?"*

A: As a parent, it's your responsibility to help your child and family to understand and solve problems. *Consider getting professional help if your child is persistently unhappy or has significant*

difficulty in adjusting to school, peers, or other family members.
Professional help may also be needed if your child is causing
you or other family members a lot of distress. You may feel that
your usual methods of managing your child aren't working or that
your child's behavior is beyond control. If your child becomes
violent when disciplined or won't cooperate with the time-out
method, then you and your child may need some direct help from
a professional counselor.

Q: *"How do I learn about professional counseling services in my
area?"*

A: It often requires a lot of effort to learn about competent
counselors and appropriate helping agencies in your community. Most pediatricians and family physicians know about local
family therapists and counselors. Ask your physician to recommend the names of at least two counselors. Some physicians
may prematurely reassure worried parents with, *"Your child is
just going through a stage"* or, *"He'll outgrow all those problems."*
Consider what your physician says, but also discuss the indica-
tions and benefits of counseling with one of the counselors.

When contacting your pediatrician or physician, you may
wish to discuss the possibility of a complete physical examination for your child before counseling begins. If your pediatrician
suggests drugs to help control your child's behavior, you might
consider getting a second opinion from another pediatrician.

Other sources of information about counselors or appropriate agencies include school principals and counselors,
teachers, the clergy, and friends. Most telephone crisis lines and
community mental health centers are also valuable sources of
information about available counseling services. Telephone
directories list psychiatrists, psychologists, marriage and family
counselors, and clinical social workers.

If your child has a learning problem at school, he should
be seen by a qualified psychologist for an evaluation which includes psychological testing. Most school systems provide a
psychological evaluation with recommendations if a child is experiencing learning or behavior problems *at school.* However,
the thoroughness of psychological evaluations provided by
schools is quite variable. Also, schools don't provide parent-child
counseling services.

Professionals who offer therapy and counseling to children
and adults, include psychiatrists (M.D.), psychologists (Ph.D.,
Psy.D., M.A., or M.S.), marriage and family counselors (Ph.D.,

M.A., or M.S.), and clinical social workers (M.S.W.). They usually belong to one or more of the following organizations.

American Association for Marriage and Family Therapy (AAMFT)
1717 K Street, N.W., Suite 407
Washington, D.C. 20026

American Family Therapy Association (AFTA)
2550 M Street, N.W., Suite 275
Washington, D.C. 20037

American Psychiatric Association (APA)
1700 18th Street, N.W.
Washington, D.C. 20009

American Psychological Association (APA)
1200 17th Street, N.W.
Washington, D.C. 20036

Association for Advancement of Behavior Therapy (AABT)
15 West 36th Street
New York, NY 10018

Association for Behavior Analysis (ABA)
Department of Psychology
Western Michigan University
Kalamazoo, MI 49008

National Association of Social Workers (NASW)
7981 Eastern Avenue
Silver Spring, MD 20910

National Register of Health Service Providers in Psychology
1200 Seventheenth Street, N.W.
Washington, D.C. 20036
      (Psychologists who apply for and meet specified standards of training and experience are listed in this national register.)

Q: *"What do I ask the family counselor during our first contact?"*

A: After obtaining the names of a couple of counselors or counseling agencies, you will need to telephone a counselor or agency. If the counselor is in *private-independent practice,* make a list of questions, and ask to speak directly with the counselor.[13] Briefly, tell the counselor the nature of your child's difficulties. Ask if he helps children with such difficulties. If not, ask whom he would recommend to help you and your child. Inquire about the training, experience, and certification he has for working with children and families. Ask about the cost of each visit, how many visits will probably be necessary, and over what period of time. When first beginning therapy and counseling, weekly visits are important.

You will be given an appointment to meet with an "intake worker" if you contact a *mental health agency* for professional services. After meeting with you and your child, the intake worker will discuss your child's difficulties with other professional staff members. The agency will decide which professional is available and qualified to help you and your child. Then the agency will set a second appointment for you to meet with your counselor.

Q: *"How do I tell my child that we are going to see a family counselor?"*

A: Use direct, simple language when telling your child that the family or the two of you are going to meet with a counselor. Be positive and tell your child that the counselor will help to solve problems. For example, you might say, *"Everyone in our family has been arguing a lot the last few months. We have an appointment with a counselor who will help us to understand our problems and to get along better."*

If your child has been receiving low grades in school, you might say, *"We're going to meet with a psychologist. She'll give you some tests, talk to you, and talk to me also. She'll offer us some ideas about how to help you with your school work and grades. We have an appointment Wednesday afternoon."*

Q: *"What should I expect when we begin counseling?"*

A: The first couple of sessions will focus on evaluation and assessment. The counselor will help evaluate and clarify the problems confronting you and your family. Since your spouse is a central part of the family, he or she should also become involved in counseling. In addition to talking with you about your child's difficulties, the counselor will ask about the expectations and goals that you have as a parent. You'll fill out brief questionnaires and keep records of your child's behavior. The counselor will talk with your child and observe you and your child together.

After *evaluating* the problems troubling you and your child, the counselor will help you to solve these difficulties. Depending upon the problems to be resolved, counselors may use one or more possible approaches.

Four approaches to helping children and parents:

- *The counselor does therapy directly with the child.* Most parents probably expect this treatment method, although this approach by itself is limited in its effectiveness.

- *The counselor teaches parents new methods for helping and managing their child.* You also may be asked to read parenting materials, perhaps *SOS!*

- *The counselor helps parents to understand and resolve their personal problems.* Such problems often include depression, life crises, or marital difficulties.

- *The counselor meets with the entire family in counseling sessions.* Some problems are best treated by working with the whole family, at one time.

Be willing to modify your expectations for counseling and be flexible in working with your counselor. However, always ask your counselor any questions that you may have about counseling. With your permission, the counselor may contact your child's teacher and recommend additional ways that the school can help your child.

Q: *"How do I pay for professional services?"*

A: Counseling costs money, but so do health care, education, transportation, family entertainment, going out to eat, and vacations. Counseling can help to reduce your child's behavioral and emotional problems and to increase his personal competence and social skills. It can improve the quality of family life.

Counselors in private-independent practice usually have a set fee for each counseling session. Community mental health agencies, however, usually charge on a sliding scale based on family income. To determine if your medical insurance might cover all or part of your expenses, check with your insurance company and talk with the counselor. If a public school system is providing psychological testing and evaluation, there won't be a charge. Your taxes pay for these services!

Main Points To Remember:
1. Family and behavior problems sometimes become difficult for parents to handle.
2. Counselors can help families to resolve problems.
3. Consider getting professional help if your usual methods of managing your child or handling family problems aren't working.

Appendices For Parents

Appendix A

Index Of Problem Behaviors With Appropriate Management Methods

PROBLEMS PARENTS FACE

"Do you want it? Hee, hee, hee!"

Does this remind you of your kids?

To use this index, look up a particular problem behavior which your child is demonstrating. Study various methods and strategies that you might use to help your child. The list, however, isn't intended to be used without first reading this book, which describes the basic principles and methods for improving behavior.

Aggression—physically aggressive actions including choking, biting, hair pulling, hitting, kicking, pinching, pushing, scratching, slapping, and spitting.
    Time-out, 57-61
    Scolding and disapproval, 44-46

Away-from-home misbehavior in outdoor play activities
>See 102
>Rewarding the alternative behavior, 26-27
>Logical consequence, 48-49
>Immediate time-out, 99
>Behavior penalty, 49-51
>Time-out for two, 117-120
>Timing-out toys and objects, 121-126
>For serious aggressive and dangerous behavior, 126-134

Baby-talk and immature language
>Accidentally rewarding the misbehavior, 9-11
>Parents agreeing on goals, 15-16
>Rewarding the alternative behavior, 26-27
>Practicing the good behavior, 27
>Active ignoring, 24-26

Back-talk, sassy talk
>Scolding and disapproval, 44-46
>Giving clear commands, 17-19
>Time-out, 57-61
>Rewarding the alternative behavior, 26-27
>Practicing the good behavior, 27
>Behavior penalty, 49-51

Bedtime problems
>Racing the timer, 142-143
>Accidentally rewarding the misbehavior, 9-11
>Rewarding the alternative behavior, 26-27
>Point-rewards and tokens, 105-111

Bedwetting, enuresis
>See 144-145
>Points for dry nights, 105-110
>Rewarding the alternative behavior, 26-27
>Daytime enuresis, 145

Chores—avoidance of tasks
>Rewarding the good behavior, 5-8, 23
>Grandma's Rule, 27-28
>Point-rewards, tokens and contracts, 105-115
>Racing the timer, 142-143
>The Resting Chair, 144

Communication problems between parent and child
>See clear communication, 15

Accidentally rewarding the misbehavior, 9-11
Time-out, 57-61
Point-rewards and tokens, 105-111
Active ignoring, 24-26
Rewarding the alternative behavior, 26-27

Appendix B

If Your Child Rebels Against Time-Out

"I'm getting out of here!"

"Escaping" from time-out may be a problem when you first begin using the time-out method. This problem can be handled, however.

Read this section if you are concerned about your child possibly rebelling against time-out. *If she resists time-out, select and follow a plan which is suited both to her age and to her particular type of rebellious behavior.*

Should your child resist time-out, you can manage this problem! Most children don't rebel beyond the first couple of weeks if their parents use time-out correctly.

Your child may be clearly angry and upset when placed in time-out. Remember, she has several purposes for displaying anger and rebellious behavior. She wants to get your attention, punish you for placing her in time-out, and try to force you to stop using time-out. Resist your child's attempts to discourage you from being an effective parent!

You have two major goals for using time-out. Your immediate goal is to abruptly stop your child's undesirable target behavior. Your long-term goal is to help your child to develop greater self-discipline and self-control. Time-out is effective in helping to achieve these goals.

Parents love their children and naturally become upset when their children are unhappy. Consequently, you and your spouse need to give help and emotional support to each other if your child becomes unhappy and hard-to-handle after being placed in time-out.

Parents should take specific steps to manage their child's resistance to time-out. If your child is *between two and four years old*, select a plan from the *first half* of this appendix to handle his rebellious behavior. If he is *between five and twelve*, select a plan from the *last half* of this appendix.

Ways Children Might Rebel Against Time-Out
And What Parents Can Do

The Two- To Four-Year-Old

Rebellion #1   **Delaying or refusing to go to time-out.**

Your Plan— Quickly carry toddlers and preschoolers to the time-out chair, even those who don't resist going to time-out. Most four-year-olds will eventually learn to walk to time-out on their own.

Rebellion #2   **Making noise in time-out.** The child may call out to his parents, cry, or have a tantrum on the time-out chair.

Your Plan A— Ignore the child. Turn away and avoid eye contact while he is in time-out. Noise-making in time-out will usually decrease by itself if the parents *consistently* ignore it.

Plan B— If the child is three or four years old, tell him that if he continues making noise you'll add minutes on the timer. If he is noisy when the timer rings, set the timer for one or two extra minutes.[56]

Comments— Noise-making is usually the only type of rebellious behavior which may continue for several weeks or longer.[67] Children try to force their parents to stop using time-out by making noise in time-out.

Rebellion #3   **"Escaping" from the time-out chair.** The child steps down from the large straight-back chair and runs off.

Your Plan A—   Retrieve the child and place him back on the chair. Stand next to the chair and harshly *command* him to stay on the chair. Say, *"Don't you dare get off that chair!"* If he continues trying to escape, consider the following alternative plans.

Plan B—   Place your hand firmly on his leg or shoulder and look away from him. Command him to stay on the chair. Say nothing else.

Plan C—   Stand behind the time-out chair and firmly hold your child on the chair. Tell him that he will be released when he stops trying to get away. Say nothing else. Before beginning this method, you must be determined to win this power struggle.

Plan D—   Firmly hold the child in your lap and sit in the chair yourself. Tell your child that you will start the timer after he stops trying to get away. You must be determined to win before beginning this method.

*Plan E—   This plan involves spanking the child if he leaves the time-out chair. The plan should not be used by parents who have trouble controlling their anger while disciplining a child.

     If the child leaves the chair, bring him back and say, *"If you get off the chair again, I will spank you."* The next time he leaves return him to the chair and give "two (and only two) spanks on the child's bottom with an open hand." Then tell him, *"If you get off the chair again, I will spank you again."* If he leaves again, return him to the chair and give only two spanks on the child's bottom with an open hand. Repeat this procedure *only* once more. *Never use this procedure*

---

*These instructions for stopping very young children from leaving a time-out chair are offered by Forehand and McMahon in *Helping The Noncompliant Child* (pp. 77-83), a book for family therapists.[27]

more than three times and always use an open hand to spank.

Comments— If the above plans are not effective, you will need to consult a family counselor regarding ways to help your child to improve his behavior. Refer to Chapter 22, "When And How To Get Professional Help."

Most children will stay on a time-out chair when commanded to do so by their parent. When escaping from time-out is a problem, most parents find that this problem rarely lasts more than one or two weeks after beginning the time-out method. Always use a large straight-back chair and a portable timer.

Rebellion #4   **Not leaving time-out after the timer rings.**

Your Plan— Tell the child that the timer rang and that it's okay to get off the chair. Then use active ignoring or leave the room.

Rebellion #5   **After leaving the time-out chair, the child con-tinues to cry or scream.**

Your Plan— If your *two- or three-year-old child* continues to scream or cry loudly after leaving time-out, walk out of the room and don't give her any attention. If your *four-year-old child* continues to cry loudly after leaving time-out, place her back in time-out for another four minutes. Do this only once.

Rebellion #6   **After leaving time-out, the child is annoyed with the parent, but does not cry or scream.**

Your Plan— Ignore your child's annoyance. Don't insist that he be pleasant after leaving time-out. He has a right to his own feelings.

Rebellion #7   **Child intentionally hurts herself while on the time-out chair.**

Comments— A child who intentionally hurts herself usually has demonstrated this same behavior at other times when disciplined. A child who hurts herself when punished has "accidentally" learned this undesirable behavior. This behavior can be changed, but you may need to work with a family counselor.* A family counselor can give you specific suggestions suited to your child.

The Five- To Twelve-Year-Old

Rebellion #1 **Delaying or refusing to go to time-out.** The child does not immediately go to time-out or refuses to go.

Your Plan— If your child delays or resists going to time-out, tell him that he must go immediately or he will have to spend additional minutes in time-out. For each ten seconds he delays going to time-out, add one more minute on the timer. *Silently* count from one to ten in order to keep track of ten seconds. Add as many as five additional minutes of time-out on the timer.

After you add five additional minutes on the timer, warn your child that he will receive a particular behavior penalty (a loss of certain privileges) if he does not immediately go to time-out.[60] After giving this warning, silently count from one to ten. If he has not gone to time-out by the time you reach ten, announce the behavior penalty and walk off. Do not count out loud, become angry, or argue. Simply walk off. See Chapter 5 for a description and examples of behavior penalty.

Consider the following example of how a mother dealt with her ten-year-old daughter, Kelly. Kelly was attempting to avoid time-out by arguing with her mother.

Mother refused to argue and said, *"Kelly, you already have ten minutes of time-out. Now you have one more minute for not going right away. That's a total of eleven minutes."* (Mother pauses and counts

---

*See Chapter 22, "When And How To Get Professional Help."

silently to ten.) *"Okay, you now have eleven minutes plus one more minute and that makes twelve minutes."* Kelly stopped arguing, turned, and reluctantly walked off to time-out.

If Kelly had continued to delay going to time-out, her mother would have added as many as five additional minutes to the original ten minutes. If Kelly had not gone to time-out by then, Mother would have announced that Kelly's privilege of watching television for the rest of the day was revoked—a behavior penalty. After announcing this particular penalty to Kelly, Mother would have walked off and refused to discuss the matter any longer. If Kelly had wanted to watch television that day, she first would have had to go to time-out for fifteen minutes.

Comments— If your child refuses to go to time-out, give her a behavior penalty. However, also permit her to go to time-out later in the day in order to remove the behavior penalty.

When you first use time-out with your child, you and your spouse should be present so that your child knows that you agree with each other. If she delays going to time-out, you might need additional practice in giving effective commands—a skill discussed in Chapter 2. Don't scold or argue with your child if she resists going to time-out. Children who resist going to time-out usually resist only the first week or two.

Rebellion #2 **Making noise in time-out.** A child may continuously call out to his parents, cry loudly, stomp his feet, say he "hates" everyone, or have a full tantrum.

Your Plan A— Ignore the child, stay away from the time-out room and "do not try to calm him down."[60] Don't scold, reassure, or answer your child. Be sure not to reward his noise-making by paying attention to this behavior. The best way to decrease noise-making is to use *active ignoring*—to withdraw all attention from your child.

Plan B— Add extra minutes on the timer for noise-making. If your child is noisy *when* the timer rings, reset the timer for two more minutes.[56]

Comments— Remember that your child's purpose for making noise is to get your attention, make you angry, and *force* you to stop using time-out. Don't get angry or scold him for making noise, as this rewards this undesirable behavior. Simply ignore him and set extra minutes on the timer. Be sure that you're using a *portable* timer so that your child doesn't learn to keep calling out to you to "see if he can come out now."

Making noise in time-out is one type of rebellious behavior which may continue for some time.[67] Many parents go to a distant part of their house or apartment to avoid the noise. Going to another part of the house until the noise stops is a good idea since this reduces stress on the parents and also ensures that the child will receive no attention.

MAKING NOISE IN TIME-OUT

"I don't like time-out!"

Some children attempt to rebel against time-out by making noise or having a tantrum. Be calm! You can handle this problem also.

Time-Out At The Motel

Although in a motel, mother and father needed to handle their six-year-old son's temper tamtrum. They placed him in time-out in their motel bathroom. However, his crying was so loud and obnoxious that they had to leave their motel room.

They found themselves standing on the sidewalk outdoors until their son's time-out was over! Mother and father correctly handled their son's noise-making by actively ignoring it.

Rebellion #3   **"Escaping" from the time-out room.** The child leaves time-out before the timer rings.

Your Plan—   For each ten seconds that the child is absent from the time-out room, she gets one more minute added to the timer, up to a maximum of five additional minutes. If she doesn't return to time-out, or is absent more than one or two minutes, she receives a behavior penalty (such as no television for the rest of the day). Refuse to get angry, announce the behavior penalty, and walk off. Don't argue with your child. Be sure to follow through with the behavior penalty which you announce.

Comments—   Escaping from time-out is usually not a problem. *If* it is a problem, it rarely lasts past the first two weeks.

Rebellion #4   **Making a mess in the time-out room.** The child may scatter objects about the room or spill water on the floor.

Your Plan—   Be matter-of-fact and require the child to clean up the mess before he may leave the room. Don't act shocked or scold.

Comments—   Recognize that making a mess in time-out is just another attempt at punishing his parents or forcing them into not using time-out. The day after placing his nine-year-old son in the bathroom for time-out, one father discovered that his new aerosol container of shaving cream was empty! His son apparently had emptied the entire container in the bathroom sink and rinsed the lather down the drain!

Rebellion #5   **Damaging the time-out room.**

Your Plan A—   The child must clean up the room and help pay for damages. One way that he may "pay" for damages is to do extra chores at home. The parent may need to select and arrange another room for time-out, a room which is safe but less easily damaged. However, do *not* use the child's bedroom.

Plan B— The parents may need to meet with a family counselor to determine specific methods to help a child who loses control when disciplined. Refer to Chapter 22, "When And How To Get Professional Help."

Rebellion #6 **Not leaving time-out after the timer rings or the child says he "likes" time-out.**

Your Plan— If the child doesn't leave time-out after the timer rings say, *"The timer rang. You can come out now if you want to, or you can stay in there—whatever you want to do."* Then turn and walk away. Say nothing else. A bright child may say that she "likes" time-out. Don't take her statement seriously. This is just another attempt at manipulating the parent into not using time-out.

Rebellion #7 **After leaving time-out, the child continues to scream, yell, and cry.**

Your Plan— Immediately place the child back into time-out for another full period of time-out.

Rebellion #8 **After leaving time-out, the child is annoyed with the parent, but does not cry or scream.**

Your Plan— Don't insist that your child be cheerful after leaving time-out. Ignore his annoyance. Be sure that you don't appear or act angry after time-out is over. Also, don't "apologize" for timing-out your son or daughter.

Rebellion #9 **Child intentionally hurts herself while in time-out.**

Comments— A child who intentionally hurts herself when angry at her parents is trying to punish them and make them feel guilty. She is attempting to manipulate her parents. This pattern of self-destructive behavior can be changed; however, you will probably need to work with a family counselor who can tailor recommendations and a plan to fit your child. Read Chapter 22, "When And How To Get Professional Help."

Parents will need professional assistance if their child physically attacks them or runs out of the house to avoid time-out. If your child day after day refuses to go to time-out and ignores the consequent behavior penalty, you may need to get professional help.

Main Point To Remember:
If your child rebels against time-out, select a plan from this appendix to effectively handle her resistance. Be sure to use a plan suited to her age.

Appendix C

Helping The Noncompliant Child To Mind—A New Program For Children Three To Seven

MISTAKES PARENTS MAKE

"It's time to get ready for school. Would you like to put away your toys?"

"NO! I'M GONNA PLAY SOME MORE!"

Give a clear command if you think that your child might ignore a simple request. Don't ask a question or make an indirect statement to your child when you want him to mind.

"No! I'm Gonna Play Some More!"

Five-year-old Benjamin is noncompliant—he fails to comply with most of his mother's requests. Mother learned from a

191

friend about a new program for helping noncompliant children who are three to seven years old. In the program the parent gives clear, effective commands and backs up those commands with time-out. The parent and child also play a special 10 minute game each day called "the child's game."

Mother wants Benjamin to get ready for school. Let's listen as she corrects her old, ineffective method of trying to get Benjamin to mind.

Mother: *"It's time to get ready for school. Would you like to put away your toys?"*

Benjamin: *"No! I'm gonna play some more!"*

Mother quickly realizes that she is asking Benjamin *if* he wants to put away his toys rather than clearly telling him to do so. She pauses and then gives a clear command.

Mother: *"You musn't be late for school. Benjamin, pick up your toys and put them in that box. Do it now!"*

Benjamin: *"No!"*

Mother silently waits about 10 seconds to give Benjamin time to obey her command. However, he continues playing with his toys. Mother then gives Benjamin an "if-then warning."

Mother: *"Benjamin, if you don't pick up your toys then you must go to time-out!"*

Benjamin: *"No!"*

Mother again waits 10 seconds to see if Benjamin is going to mind. Since he doesn't obey, she places him in time-out.

Mother: *"Time-out for not minding! Benjamin, go now!"*

Benjamin: *"Waaah! I don't wanna go to time-out!"*

Mother says nothing more and leads Benjamin to time-out. She also places a ticking timer nearby so he can hear it ring. After five minutes the timer rings, and Benjamin comes out.

Mother: *"Benjamin, you must pick up your toys now!"*

Benjamin: *"I'm gonna put them all together in the box. I'm gonna play with them after school."*

Mother: *"I'm glad that you put your toys away, Benjamin. Good for you!"*

Good for mother! She is realizing that sometimes she must give clear, effective commands if she expects Benjamin to mind. Benjamin will learn that he gets praise for minding and time-out for not minding. He will gradually learn to obey clear commands without mother using time-out.

Parents whose children are between three and seven years old may use a special program to teach their children to mind.[27,66] This program has been used at the University of Georgia, Idaho State University, the University of British Columbia, and at many parent-child counseling centers.*

Play "the child's game" with your son or daughter for 10 minutes each day. Tell your child to choose a game and that you will play it with him. After he selects an activity, give him your undivided attention and do only what he wants to do. Don't make suggestions, give commands, ask questions, or try to teach him something while playing this special game. If he decides to change the game, that's fine, but be sure that *you* don't change or direct the game. Give your child lots of attention and frequently praise any good behavior you observe. *Actively ignore any minor misbehavior* during this special activity. If your child engages in aggressive or dangerous misbehavior, discontinue the child's game. Handle the misbehavior with a scolding, a warning, or time-out. Then continue playing the child's game if he wishes to do so.

Your child will love the extra attention, and playing the game together will improve and strengthen your relationship. You will get additional experience rewarding his good behavior and ignoring his bad behavior. Play the child's game each day for at least a week or two *before* you begin the discipline part of the child compliance program. Then continue playing this game daily. Remember, never give your child criticism or commands while you are playing the child's game unless he acts aggressively or dangerously.

When Mother played the child's game with five-year-old Benjamin, he usually wanted her to sit on the floor next to him and help build things out of Tinker Toys and Lincoln Logs. Playing the child's game is an important part of the child compliance program. Don't skip it.

Use the following five discipline steps to teach your child to mind you.

1. When your son or daughter is likely to ignore or disobey your instructions, give a clear command. Say, *"Benjamin, pick up your toys and put them in that box. Do it now!"* Don't ask a question

---

*This child compliance program is described by Forehand and McMahon in *Helping The Noncompliant Child,* a book for family therapists.[27]

or give vague instructions. You may wish to review "How to give effective commands" in Chapter 2. If you find that you have given vague instructions, it's easy to correct yourself. Simply pause, say your child's name, get eye contact, and then give a clear command.

Be sure that you are asking your child to do a *simple task,* such as *"pick up your shoes"* or *"take your cereal bowl to the sink."* Don't give him a more complex task, such as *"straighten your room"* or *"practice the piano."*

Only give a command that you are willing to take the time to enforce. If you don't have sufficient time to follow through, then give your child a simple *request* rather than a *command.*

2. Wait 10 seconds and continue looking at your child. If he starts to obey your command, give him praise and attention. If he doesn't obey, go to Step Three.

3. Give your child an "if-then warning." Say, *"Benjamin, if you don't pick up your toys, then you must go to time-out!"*

4. Wait another 10 seconds and continue looking at your child. If he obeys your if-then warning give him praise and attention. If he doesn't obey your warning, quickly place him in time-out. Say, *"Time-out for not minding! Benjamin, go now!"* At this point, he must go to time-out even if he begins picking up his toys or begs for a third chance. If you think that you might have difficulty placing your child in time-out read Appendix B, which tells how to get a rebellious child to cooperate with the time-out method.

5. After time-out is over, return your child to the same task that he earlier refused to do. Say, *"Benjamin, you must pick up your toys now!"* If he minds, give him praise. If he doesn't mind, again follow the above steps, beginning with Step Two. Repeat these steps if necessary.[66] If the steps are properly followed, it's unusual to have to repeat them.

Main Points To Remember:
1. Play "the child's game" for 10 minutes each day.
2. Give clear instructions and commands when you want your child to mind.
3. Teach your child to follow your commands by using all five discipline steps, if needed.

Appendix D

Quizzes And Answers For Parents

Each quiz asks 10 questions over a different section of *SOS!* Test your knowledge of the methods and skills described in *SOS!* by marking the correct answers. Then check your answers with those given at the end of each quiz.

Quiz One

Chapter 1. "Why Kids Behave And Misbehave"

Chapter 2. "Clear Communication Promotes Effective Parenting"

Quiz Two

Chapter 3. "Ways Of Increasing Good Behavior"

Chapter 5. "Major Methods For Stopping Bad Behavior"

Quiz Three

Chapter 4. "What Is Time-Out? When Do Parents Use It?"

Chapters 6 through 12. "Basic Skills Of The Time-Out Method"

Appendix B. "If Your Child Rebels Against Time-Out"

Quiz Four

Chapters 13 through 18. "Further Applications Of Your
                                        Parenting Skills"

Patrice Nolan helped to construct the quiz items.

Appendix D

Quizzes And Answers For Parents

QUIZ ONE
Covering:
Chapter 1. ''Why Kids Behave And Misbehave''
Chapter 2. ''Clear Communication Promotes Effective Parenting''

Select the best answer to each question.

1. When you reward any behavior, that behavior will:
   a. occur more often in the future.
   b. occur less often in the future.
   c. not change at all.
   d. stop occurring immediately.

2. When praising a child, it's best to:
   a. give the child money along with praise.
   b. not praise too often.
   c. praise the specific behavior.
   d. all of the above are correct.

3. An error or mistake commonly made by parents is:
   a. rewarding good behavior.
   b. punishing some bad behavior.
   c. rewarding good behavior quickly.
   d. failing to reward good behavior.

4. Mike's tantrum in the grocery store earned him a candy bar. Mike's mother committed which error?
   a. failed to reward good behavior.
   b. accidentally punished good behavior.
   c. accidentally rewarded bad behavior. .
   d. all of the above are correct.

5. Parents should manage their child by:
   a. rewarding good behavior.
   b. not accidentally rewarding bad behavior.
   c. using mild punishment for some bad behavior.
   d. all of the above.

6. A parent gives a command when:
   a. the parent wants the child to stop or start a behavior but believes that a request will be disobeyed.
   b. a simple request will be obeyed.
   c. anytime a parent wants a child to stop a behavior.
   d. anytime a parent wants a child to start a behavior.

7. Clear communication between parents and between parent and child leads to:
   a. agreement on "house rules."
   b. fewer discipline problems.
   c. better parenting.
   d. all of the above are correct.

8. A "house rule" that has been set up by *both parents and children:*
   a. is *more* likely to be followed by the child.
   b. is *less* likely to be followed by the child.
   c. shouldn't be enforced by the parents.

9. *"Put the cookie back!"* is an example of:
   a. saying the child's name.
   b. keeping the command simple.
   c. backing up the command.
   d. a stern facial expression.

10. *"Look at him! He's always into something! I must be a bad, terrible parent."* This was probably said by:
    a. an angry parent.
    b. a hopeless parent.
    c. a guilty parent.
    d. a low energy parent.

ANSWER | | | a c d c d a d a b c
QUESTION 1. 2. 3. 4. 5. 6. 7. 8. 9. 10.

Quizzes And Answers For Parents

QUIZ TWO
Covering:
Chapter 3. "Ways Of Increasing Good Behavior"
Chapter 5. "Major Methods For Stopping Bad Behavior"

Select the best answer to each question.

1. Bill's parents actively ignore his sarcasm. They also praise him when he speaks politely. Bill's parents are:
    a. rewarding teasing.
    b. modeling bad behavior.
    c. rewarding good alternative behavior.
    d. all of the above are correct.

2. Grandma's Rule simply says:
    a. never punish a child.
    b. the pleasant activity comes *after* the chore.
    c. the pleasant activity comes *before* the chore.
    d. give grandchildren lots of cookies!

3. Diana's dad taught Diana how to play with the new puppy without hurting the animal. Diana's father was:
    a. punishing Diana for mistreating the puppy.
    b. helping Diana practice good behavior.
    c. using Grandma's Rule.
    d. using active ignoring.

4. We increase our child's good behavior by:
    a. rewarding those behaviors.
    b. using active ignoring for some misbehavior.
    c. helping the child to practice good behavior.
    d. all of the above.

5. Actively ignoring a whining child:
    a. will reward the whining behavior.
    b. will not change the child's behavior.
    c. will reduce the whining behavior in the long run.
    d. is impossible to do.

6. Any mild punishment will be more effective if:
    a. parents only threaten to use it.
    b. no reason is given for the punishment.
    c. parents remember to also praise the good alternative behavior.
    d. all of the above are correct.

7. Scolding is *not* an effective mild punishment if your child:
    a. talks back to you when being scolded.
    b. ignores you or smiles when being scolded.
    c. has a temper tantrum when being scolded.
    d. all of the above are correct answers.

8. When Mary broke her little sister's doll, her parents gave one of Mary's dolls to the little sister. This is an example of:
    a. logical consequence.
    b. natural consequence.
    c. time-out.
    d. all of the above.

9. Tom lost his TV privileges because he stayed out past his curfew. This is:
    a. logical consequence.
    b. natural consequence.
    c. behavior penalty.
    d. scolding and disapproval.

10. Bad behavior may continue because:
    a. the rewards for the bad behavior outweigh the punishment.
    b. the parents model or demonstrate the bad behavior themselves.
    c. parents rarely follow through with the mild punishment.
    d. all of the above.

ANSWER | | c b b d c c d a c d
QUESTION 1. 2. 3. 4. 5. 6. 7. 8. 9. 10.

Quizzes And Answers For Parents

QUIZ THREE
Covering:
Chapter 4. "What Is Time-Out? When Do Parents Use It?"
Chapters 6 through 12. "Basic Skills Of The Time-Out Method"
Appendix B. "If Your Child Rebels Against Time-Out"

Select the best answer to each question.

1. After time-out is over, parents should ask their child:
   a. *"Do you still love Mommy and Daddy?"*
   b. *"Can you say you're sorry?"*
   c. *"Will you promise to be good?"*
   d. *"Why did you have to go to time-out?"*

2. Time-out is an effective way to reduce misbehaviors for children aged:
   a. one to five years old.
   b. two to twelve years old.
   c. six to twelve years old.
   d. ten to sixteen years old.

3. Time-out *isn't* very useful in reducing:
   a. behaviors not seen by the parents.
   b. mocking or sassing parents.
   c. toy grabbing.
   d. spitting at others.

4. The best time for demonstrating and explaining time-out to your child is:
   a. while you or your child is angry.
   b. before you ever use time-out.
   c. while you are using time-out for the first time.
   d. all of the above.

5. The place chosen for time-out should be:
   a. dull, boring, and safe.
   b. the child's bedroom.
   c. a frightening place.
   d. where the child's toys are.

6. A timer is a necessary part of time-out because:
   a. timers can't "forget" the child.
   b. children take responsibility for correctly leaving time-out.
   c. ticking timers let others know that "time-out is in progress."
   d. all of the above are correct.

7. *"David! I can't believe that you're teasing your sister again! Go to time-out—this time for 20 minutes!"* David's father just made which error?
   a. only threatening to use time-out.
   b. using a very long period of time-out.
   c. not selecting the right place for time-out.
   d. all of the above.

8. If your child screams during time-out, you should:
   a. scold the child for being noisy.
   b. stop using time-out.
   c. ignore the noise or add one to three minutes to time-out if he's noisy when the timer rings.
   d. give the child a behavior penalty or spanking.

9. When a child is annoyed with her parents after being in time-out, her parents should:
   a. apologize for using time-out.
   b. ignore her complaints and realize that she has a right to her feelings.
   c. put her back into time-out.
   d. offer her a candy bar or ice cream!

10. During the first few weeks of using time-out, parents should expect their son to:
    a. completely stop misbehaving.
    b. go to time-out without any fussing or complaining.
    c. apologize for his misbehavior.
    d. "test" and challenge his parents' new method of discipline.

ANSWER —
QUESTION —
1. d
2. b
3. a
4. b
5. a
6. d
7. b
8. c
9. b
10. d

Quizzes And Answers For Parents

QUIZ FOUR
Covering:
Chapters 13 through 18. "Further Applications Of Your
Parenting Skills"

Select the best answer to each question.

1. Tokens and point-rewards may be exchanged for:
   a. praise.
   b. freedom from time-out.
   c. special privileges or inexpensive toys.
   d. all of the above.

2. The best and easiest way to improve behavior is to:
   a. reward good behavior.
   b. punish bad behavior.
   c. use time-out.
   d. worry and fret a lot!

3. A parent-child contract should be written down and include:
   a. duties of the child only.
   b. everyone's duties and consequences if the contract isn't upheld.
   c. no possibility for changing the contract.
   d. only the parents' signature.

4. Timing-out both children reduces fighting because:
   a. both children get the same mild punishment.
   b. parents aren't rewarding children with attention by scolding them.
   c. parents don't have to decide which child is guilty and which is innocent.
   d. all of the above are correct.

5. An aggressive child's threats to injure another child should:
   a. result in time-out.
   b. be ignored.
   c. lead to a spanking.
   d. be given a lot of attention.

6. Reflective listening requires a parent to:
   a. give the child attention when he expresses feelings.
   b. restate the child's feelings and the situation that the child describes.
   c. give advice or suggestions only *after* the child has expressed his feelings.
   d. all of the above.

7. Point-reward calendars are effective because:
   a. children earn points for misbehaving.
   b. children can buy rewards with points earned.
   c. parents don't have to give praise.
   d. all of the above are correct.

8. Before using time-out in public or when visiting friends:
   a. the child should be accustomed to time-out at home.
   b. parents should tell the child how she is expected to behave in public.
   c. parents should be prepared to deal with interference from others.
   d. all of the above.

9. When two children keep fighting over a toy, a parent should:
   a. scold them into taking turns.
   b. put either the children or the toy in time-out.
   c. give the toy to a charity.
   d. buy each child a new toy.

10. Reflective listening requires the parent to:
    a. scold the child if the child voices irrational plans.
    b. offer suggestions only *before* the child has expressed his feelings.
    c. offer suggestions only *after* the child has expressed his feelings.
    d. all of the above are correct.

ANSWER — — c a b d a d b d b c

QUESTION — 1. 2. 3. 4. 5. 6. 7. 8. 9. 10.

Appendices For Professionals

Appendix E

Professionals Using *SOS!*

SOS! teaches principles of behavior and specific methods and skills for improving the behavior of children. The goal of *SOS!* is to help parents to be better parents. Professionals who counsel parents, teach students, or render social services to families will find *SOS!* an interesting and useful teaching tool.

Theoretical Trends In Parent Training-Education

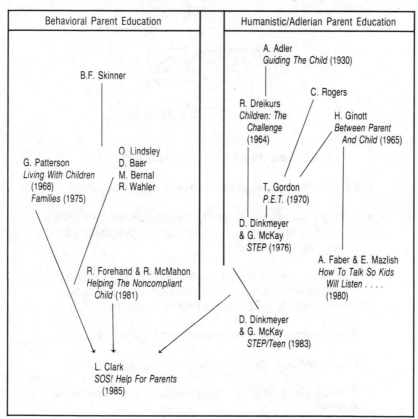

The two dominant theoretical systems in parent education are the behavioral and the humanistic/Adlerian approaches. The figure "Theoretical Trends In Parent Training-Education" shows the interchange of ideas within each of these two systems. The figure also shows the development of *SOS!*

Professionals familiar with the Adlerian *STEP*[18] parenting handbook may recognize similarity in the art work between *STEP* and *SOS!* John Robb, a Denver artist, did the illustrations for both books. All captions for *SOS!* illustrations were written by the author.

Research indicates that media materials can teach parenting skills such as time-out.[38] *SOS!* is intended to stimulate additional research on the effectiveness of printed materials teaching child management skills when used alone and when used as a tool by family counselors.

SOS! Help For Parents is suggested for:

- Family therapists, social service professionals.

- Colleges—courses in family therapy, behavior therapy, child development, parenting, special education, practicum, field placements.

- Parenting programs presented at community centers, social service agencies, churches and synagogues, mental health and counseling centers, preschools.

- Elementary teachers, special education classes.

- Kindergartens, preschools, day-care centers.

- Special programs for handicapped and "high risk" children.

- Pediatricians, hospitals.

A useful kit of parent education/counseling aids, *SOS! Help For Professionals*, is available. The supplementary materials are intended for professionals who offer parent education classes or parent counseling. See order form on page 246.

The following materials are included in the *SOS! Help For Professionals* kit:

- One copy of **SOS! Help For Parents** book.

- One copy of **How To Use Time-Out Effectively** audiotape (Revised; 60 plus minutes), demonstrates and teaches time-out skills. Also, two children tell their feelings about time-out. Suitable for individual or group listening.

- Basic Child Rearing Methods: 16 flip-over cards with enlarged cartoon illustrations (8 1/2" by 11" bound cards) illustrate and teach effective parenting skills. Suitable for use with individuals or groups.

- Basic Time-Out Steps: 11 flip-over cards with enlarged cartoon illustrations (8 1/2" by 11" bound cards) illustrate and teach time-out skills. Coordinated with above audiotape and book.

- Time-Out Parent Inventory (TOPI). Reproducible Record Form and Manual. Assesses the time-out skills of parents. (reliability r= .89)

- Parent Handouts. Reproducible handouts illustrate and teach child management skills.

- Quizzes for parents. Reproducible multiple-choice quizzes ask questions over sections of SOS! Help For Parents. Includes answer sheet and scoring key.

- Professional Manual provides suggested outlines for teaching parenting skills described in SOS! Help For Parents.

- Other materials.

Appendix F

More Parent Education And Parent Counseling Resources For Professionals

This appendix describes additional resources for professionals who offer parent education classes and parent counseling. Both the behavioral and humanistic/Adlerian approaches present methods, materials, and training programs in parenting. The behavioral approach is producing impressive research data, documenting its effectiveness. The following figure shows some major differences between the behavioral and the humanistic/Adlerian approaches to parent education.

Differences Between Behavioral And Humanistic/Adlerian Systems Of Parent Education

		System	
	Differences	*Behavioral*	*Humanistic/Adlerian*
1.	Method of research	Systematic observation, recording, and control of behavior; data-based	Case histories, anecdotes
2.	Democratic emphasis in parenting	Less emphasis	More emphasis
3.	Who can benefit?	Parents and children at *all* levels of adjustment and functioning	Parents and children at higher levels of adjustment and functioning
4.	Communication of feelings between parent and child	Less emphasis	More emphasis

The following books offer basic information for students and professionals regarding the *behavioral* approach.

Gelfand, D.M., & Hartman, D.P. (1984). *Child Behavior Analysis And Therapy.* (2nd ed.). NY: Pergamon Press.
Martin, G., & Pear, J. (1983). *Behavior Modification: What Is It And How To Do It.* (2nd ed.). Englewood Cliffs, NJ: Prentice-Hall.

Useful books for professionals which describe issues and methods in behavioral parent education include the following:

Polster, R.A., & Dangel, R.F. (Eds.). (1984). *Parent Training: Foundations Of Research And Practice.* NY: Guilford Press.
Forehand, R.L., & McMahon, R.J. (1981). *Helping The Noncompliant Child.* NY: Guilford Press.
Dangel, R.F., & Polster, R.A. (in press). *Teaching Child Management Skills.* NY: Pergamon Press.

"Consumer Issues In Parent Training," a chapter in *Parent Training: Foundations Of Research And Practice,* provides an interesting overview of *behavioral* parent education.[9]

Winning! Child Management Skills[15] is one of the most extensive (and expensive!) behavioral parent education programs available to professionals. It includes a series of video training tapes which can be used with individuals or groups. For information write, *Winning!,* P.O. Box 32, Arlington, TX 76004.

Several companies publish a variety of parent education materials including books, audio tapes, video tapes, films, and "packaged" training programs. They also offer materials for professionals who conduct in-service training programs for teachers. American Guidance Service produces humanistic/Adlerian parent education materials including *STEP* and *STEP/Teen.* The other companies offer behavioral parent training materials for professionals. Consider asking for a catalog of parent education and parent counseling materials from the following publishers.

Research Press
Box 31779
Champaign, IL 61821

American Guidance Service
Publishers' Building
Circle Pines, MN 55014-1796

Castalia Publishing Co.
P.O. Box 1587
Eugene, OR 97440

PRO-ED
5341 Industrial Oaks Blvd.
Austin, TX 78735
(Owner of H&H Enterprises)

REFERENCES

1   Alberto, P.A., & Troutman, A.C. (1982). *Applied behavior analysis for teachers.* Columbus, OH: Charles Merrill Publishing Company.
2   Allen, J. (1984). *What do I do when?* San Luis Obispo, CA: Impact Publishers.
3   American Psychiatric Association. (1980). *Diagnostic and statistical manual of mental disorders.* (3rd ed.). Washington, DC: Author.
4   Azrin, N.H., & Besalel, V.A. (1979). *A parent's guide to bedwetting control.* NY: Pocket Books.
5   Baker, J.G., Stanish, B., & Fraser, B. (1972). Comparative effects of a token economy in nursery school. *Mental Retardation, 10,* 16-19. (From Psychological Abstracts, 1973, *49,* Abstract No: 03092)
6   Bandura, A., & Walters, R.H. (1963). *Social learning and personality development.* NY: Holt, Rinehart & Winston.
7   Barkley, R.A. (1981). *Hyperactive children: A handbook for diagnosis and treatment.* NY: Guilford Press.
8   Becker, W.C. (1971). *Parents are teachers: A child management program.* Champaign, IL: Research Press.
9   Bernal, M.E. (1984). Consumer issues in parent training. In R.F. Dangel & R.A. Polster (Eds.), *Parent training: Foundations of research and practice.* (pp. 477-546). NY: Guilford Press.
10 Bernal, M.E., & North, J.A. (1978). A survey of parent training manuals. *Journal of Applied Behavior Analysis, 11,* 533-544.
11 Blackham, G.J., & Silberman, A. (1980). *Modification of child and adolescent behavior.* (3rd ed.). Belmont, CA: Wadsworth Publishing Co.
12 Bureau of Education for Exceptional Children, Kentucky Department of Education. (1971). *a.b.c's of a parent-teacher conference.* Frankfort, KY: Author.
13 Christophersen, E.R. (1982). *Little people.* (2nd ed.). Lawrence, KS: H&H Enterprises.
14 Clark, L.F. (1972). *Time out and 10-10-10.* Unpublished manuscript.
15 Dangel, R.F., & Polster, R.A. (1984). Winning!: A systematic, empirical approach to parent training. In R.F. Dangel & R.A. Polster (Eds.), *Parent training: Foundations of research and practice.* (pp. 162-201). NY: Guilford Press.
16 Dangel, R.F., & Polster, R.A. (in press). *Teaching child management skills.* NY: Pergamon Press.
17 DeRisi, W.J., & Butz, G. (1975). *Writing behavioral contracts: A case simulation practice manual.* Champaign, IL: Research Press.
18 Dinkmeyer, D., & McKay, G. (1976). *The parent's handbook: Systematic training for effective parenting.* Circle Pines, MN: American Guidance Service.
19 Dinkmeyer, D., & McKay, G. (1983). *The parent's guide: STEP/Teen.* Circle Pines, MN: American Guidance Service.
20 Dreikurs, R., & Grey, L. (1968). *A parents' guide to child discipline.* NY: Hawthorn Books.

21   Dreikurs, R., & Soltz, V. (1964), *Children: The challenge.* NY: Hawthorn.
22   Dullaart-Pruyser, E. (1977). Operant conditioning with autistic children:
     A survey of the literature. *Nederlands Tijdsehrift voor de
     Psychologic en haar Grensqebieden, 32,* 307-332. (From
     Psychological Abstracts, 1979, *61,* Abstract No: 04175)
23   Egan, G. (1982). *The skilled helper: Models, skills, and methods for ef-
     fective helping.* (2nd ed.). Monterey, CA: Brooks/Cole Publishing
     Company.
24   Eimers, R., & Aitchison, R. (1977). *Effective parents/responsible children.*
     NY: McGraw-Hill Book Co.
25   Faber, A., & Mazlish, E. (1980). *How to talk so kids will listen & listen
     so kids will talk.* NY: Avon.
26   Forehand, R.L., & King, E. (1974). Pre-school children's noncompliance:
     Effects of short-term behavior therapy. *Journal of Community
     Psychology, 2,* 42-44.
27   Forehand, R.L., & McMahon, R.J. (1981). *Helping the noncompliant child.*
     NY: Guilford Press.
28   Gast, D.L., & Nelson, C.M. (1977). Legal and ethical considerations for
     the use of timeout in special education settings. *Journal of Special
     Education, 11,* 457-467.
29   Gazda, G.M., Asbury, F.R., Balzer, F.J., Childers, W.C., & Walters, R.P.
     (1977). *Human relations development: A manual for educators.*
     (2nd ed.). Boston, Allyn and Bacon.
30   Gelfand, D.M., & Hartman, D.P. (1984). *Child behavior analysis and
     therapy.* (2nd ed.) NY: Pergamon Press.
31   Ginott, H. (1965). *Between parent and child.* NY: Avon.
32   Ginott, H. (1971). *Between parent and teenager.* NY: Avon.
33   Gordon, T. (1970). *P.E.T.: Parent effectiveness training.* NY: Plume.
34   Gottwald, P. (1975). Response contingent time out: An examination of
     outcome data. *European Journal of Behavioural Analysis &
     Modification, 1,* 1-16. (From *Psychological Abstracts,* 1976, *56,*
     Abstract No: 01061)
35   Gottwald, P., & Redlin, W. (1972). Behavior therapy with mentally
     handicapped children: Basic concepts, results and problems of
     behavior therapy with retarded, autistic and schizophrenic
     children. *Zeitschrift fur Klinische Psychologic, 2,* 93-149. (From
     Psychological Abstracts, 1974, *51,* Abstract No: 07691)
36   Hall, R.V., & Hall, M.C. (1980). *How to use time out.* Lawrence, KS: H&H
     Enterprises.
37   Hall, R.V., & Hall, M.C. (1982). *How to negotiate a behavioral contract.*
     Lawrence, KS: H&H Enterprises.
38   Hansen, D.J., Tisdelle, D.A., & O'Dell, S.L. (1984). Teaching parents time-
     out with media materials: The importance of observation and feed-
     back. *Child and Adolescent Psychiatry, 1,* 20-25.
39   Harris, T. (1967). *I'm ok—You're ok.* NY: Avon.
40   Hobbs, S.A., & Forehand, R. (1977). Important parameters in the use
     of timeout with children: A re-examination. *Journal of Behavior
     Therapy and Experimental Psychiatry, 8,* 365-370.
41   Hobbs, S.A., Forehand, R., & Murray, R.G. (1978). Effects of various dura-
     tions of timeout on the noncompliant behavior of children. *Behavior
     Therapy, 9,* 652-659.

42 Laird, R. (February, 1984). Personal communication.
43 Lambert, J.L. (1976). Perseveration responses and discrimination learning among mentally retarded subjects. *Enfance, 4,* 425-446. (From *Psychological Abstracts, 1978, 60,* Abstract No: 03317)
44 Lindsley, O.R. (1966). An experiment with parents handling behavior at home. *Johnstone Bulletin, 9,* 27-36.
45 Lupercio, L., & Ribes, E. (1976). Comparative effects of extinction and time-out of reinforcement on imitative behavior. *Revista Mexicana de Analisis de la Conducta, 2,* 42-53. (From *Psychological Abstracts, 1979, 61,* Abstract No: 13135)
46 Madsen, C.H. & Madsen, C.K. (1981). *Teaching/Discipline: A positive approach for educational development.* (3rd ed.). Boston, Allyn and Bacon.
47 Marks, I.M., Cameron, P.M., & Silberfeld, M. (1971). Operant therapy for an abnormal personality. *British Medical Journal, 1,* 647-648. (From *Psychological Abstracts, 1972, 47,* Abstract No: 04981)
48 Martin, G., & Pear, J. (1983). *Behavior modification: What it is and how to do it.* Englewood Cliffs, NJ: Prentice-Hall, Inc.
49 Mason, D. (1983). How to grow a parents' group. *Parents, 60,* 194-200.
50 Matson, J.L., & Dilorenzo, T.M. (1984). *Punishment and its alternatives: A new perspective for behavior modification.* NY: Springer Publishing Co.
51 Miller, W.H. (1975). *Systematic parent training: Procedures, cases, and issues.* Champaign, IL: Research Press.
52 Nolan, P. (December, 1984). Personal communication.
53 Nordlund, O., & Ronnberg, S. (1977). Treatment of a child with disruptive behaviors during his mother's social contact. *Scandinavian Journal of Behavior Therapy, 6,* 19-24. (From *Psychological Abstracts, 1978, 59,* Abstract No: 03892)
54 Oshio, C., Tomiyasu, Y., & Komiya, M. (1974). Shaping appropriate eating behavior of a profoundly retarded boy. *Japanese Journal of Special Education, 12,* 1-9. (From *Psychological Abstracts, 1975, 53,* Abstract No: 12530)
55 Osmon, B. (1979). *Learning disabilities: A family affair.* NY: Random House.
56 Patterson, G.R. (1975). *Families: Applications of social learning to family life.* Champaign, IL: Research Press.
57 Patterson, G.R. (1976). *Living with children: New methods for parents and teachers.* Champaign, IL: Research Press.
58 Patterson, G.R. (1976). The aggressive child: Victim and architect of a coercive system. In E.J. Mash, L.A. Hamerlynck & L.C. Handy (Eds.), *Behavior modification and families.* (pp. 267-316). NY: Brunner/Mazel.
59 Patterson, G.R. (1982). *A social learning approach. Vol. 3. Coercive family process.* Eugene, OR: Castalia Publishing Co.
60 Patterson, G.R. (Speaker), (1982). *Time-out!* (Videocassette). Eugene, OR: Castalia Publishing Company.
61 Patterson, G.R. (1984, November). *Prevention of antisocial behavior: A problem in three levels.* Paper presented at the meeting of Association for Advancement of Behavior Therapy, Philadelphia, PA. The term "nattering" was coined by J. Reid.

62   Patterson, G.R., & Forgatch, M. (Producers). (1975). *Family living series: Part I* (Audiocassette program No. 0026). Champaign, IL: Research Press.
63   Polster, R.A., & Dangel, R.F. (Eds.). (1984). *Parent training: Foundations of research and practice.* NY: Guilford Press.
64   Premack, D. (1959). Toward empirical behavior laws: 1. positive reinforcement. *Psychological Review, 66,* 219-233.
65   Ribes, I., Emilio, et al. (1970). Use of punishment in the behavior modification of retarded children. *Revista Latinoamericana de Psicologia, 2,* 137-159. (From *Psychological Abstracts, 1971, 45,* Abstract No: 06495)
66   Roberts, M.W. (1982). *Parent handouts 1,2,3.* (Available from Mark Roberts, Idaho State University, Pocatello, ID.)
67   Roberts, M.W. (1982). Resistance to timeout: Some normative data. *Behavioral Assessment, 4,* 237-246.
68   Roberts, M. (December, 28, 1984). Personal communication.
69   Roberts, M.W. McMahon, R.J., Forehand, R., & Humphreys, L. (1978). The effect of parental instruction-giving on child compliance. *Behavior Therapy, 9,* 793-798.
70   Rodriguez Rueda, L. (1978). Modification of the incorrect production of phonemes in retarded children. *Aprendizaje y comportamiento, 1,* 45-59. (From *Psychological Abstracts, 1980, 64,* Abstract No: 12876)
71   Schaefer, C.E. (1979). *Childhood encopresis and enuresis: Causes and therapy.* NY: Van Nostrand Reinhold.
72   Scott, E.A. (1977). Treatment of encopresis in a classroom setting: A case study. *British Journal of Educational Psychology, 47,* 199-202. (From *Psychological Abstracts, 1978, 60,* Abstract No: 01944)
73   Skinner, B.F. (1953). *Science and human behavior.* NY: Macmillan.
74   Steeves, J.M., Martin, G.L., & Pear, J.J. (1970). Self-imposed time-out by autistic children during an operant training program. *Behavior Therapy, 1,* 371-381. (From *Psychological Abstracts, 1972, 47,* Abstract No: 09390)
75   Sulzer-Azaroff, B., & Mayer, G.R. (1977). *Applying behavior-analysis procedures with children and youth.* NY: Holt, Rinehart and Winston.
76   Wagonseller, B.R., Burnett, M., Salzberg, B., & Burnett, J. (1977). *The art of parenting kit: A complete training kit.* (Filmstrip and audiocassette kit No. 1810). Champaign, IL: Research Press.
77   Wilson, G.T., & O'Leary, K.D. (1980). *Principles of behavior therapy.* Englewood Cliffs, NJ: Prentice-Hall, Inc.
78   Wright, L. (1978). *Parent power: A guide to responsible child-rearing.* NY: Psychological Dimensions, Inc.

Tear-Out Sheets For Parents And Teachers

Basic Child Rearing Rules And Errors

What can you do to help your child improve his or her behavior? *Follow three basic child rearing rules and avoid four possible errors.* These rules and errors are discussed in Chapter 1 of *SOS! Help For Parents.*

Three Child Rearing Rules—
Parents' Check List

Rule #1. Reward good behavior (and do it quickly and often).*

Rule #2. Don't "accidentally" reward bad behavior.**

Rule #3. Punish some bad behavior (but use *mild* punishment only).

"Accidentally" Causing Behavior Problems—
Four Child Rearing *Errors To Avoid*

Error #1. Parents fail to reward good behavior.

Error #2. Parents "accidentally" punish good behavior.

Error #3. Parents "accidentally" reward bad behavior.

Error #4. Parents fail to punish bad behavior (when *mild* punishment is indicated).

---

*When behavior is rewarded, that behavior receives "positive reinforcement" or simply "reinforcement."
**When behavior which once was rewarded is no longer rewarded, the term "extinction" is used. Extinction is also called nonreinforcement of behavior.

Rewards Children Like

"That's great! You're learning to tie your own shoes!"

It's important to reward your child's good behavior. Rewarding good behavior is the easiest and best way to improve behavior. What rewards should parents use? *Rewards that motivate children are social rewards, activity rewards, and material rewards.*

Rewards Children Like

Social Rewards	Activity Rewards Including Privileges	Material Rewards
Smiles	Play cards with mother	Ice cream
Hugs	Go to park	Ball
Pats	Look at book with father	Money
Attention	Help bake cookies	Book
Touching	Watch a late TV movie	Jump rope
Clap hands	Have a friend over	Balloons
Winks	Play ball with father	Yo-yo
Praise	Play a game together	Flashlight
"Good job"	Go out for pizza together	Record

It's also important to "fail to reward" your child's bad behavior. If you "accidentally" reward bad behavior, you will strengthen that bad behavior.

Reward only good behavior and do it quickly and often. Basic child rearing rules and common errors are discussed in Chapter 1 of *SOS! Help For Parents.*

How To Give Effective Instructions And Commands To Your Child

All parents must be able to give clear, effective instructions and commands on occasion. They must also be able to "back up" their commands. A command is a request to immediately start or stop a behavior.

When are commands given? Give your child a command when you want him to *stop* a specific misbehavior *and* you believe that he might disobey a simple request to stop the misbehavior. Also, give a command when you want your child to *start* a particular behavior *and* you believe that your child might disobey a simple request to start the behavior:

How should you give a command? Follow the guidelines listed below:

Giving Effective Commands To Your Child

Parents' Check List

✔		Steps To Follow:
	1.	Move close to your child.
	2.	Have a stern facial expression.
	3.	Say his or her name.
	4.	Get and *maintain* eye contact.
	5.	Use a firm tone of voice.
	6.	Give a direct, simple, and clear command.
	7.	"Back up" your command if necessary.

JOHN ROBB

Be sure to give "good" instructions and commands rather than "bad" instructions and commands. "Good" commands are clear, direct, and simple. "Bad" commands are unclear, indirect, vague, complicated, consist of chains of commands, or are given as questions.

What if your child doesn't obey your command? You have *time-out*—a useful back-up! The correct steps for using time-out and how to give effective commands are described in *SOS! Help For Parents*.

Basic Steps For *Initially* Using Time-Out—
Parents' Check List

_____✔_____ Steps To Follow:

_____ 1. Select one target behavior on which to use time-out. (Chapter 4)

_____ *2. Count how often this target behavior occurs. (Chapter 4)

_____ 3. Pick out a boring place for time-out. (Chapter 7)

_____ 4. Explain time-out to your child. (Chapter 8)

_____ 5. Wait patiently for the target behavior to occur. (Chapter 9)

TARGET BEHAVIOR OCCURS!

_____ 6. Place your child in the time-out place and use no more than 10 words and 10 seconds. (Chapter 9)

_____ 7. Get the portable timer, set it to ring in _____ minutes, and place it within hearing distance of your child. (Chapter 10)

_____ 8. Wait for the timer to ring—remove all attention from your child while she waits for the timer to ring. (Chapter 10)

_____ *9. Ask your child, after the timer rings, why she was sent to time-out. (Chapter 11)

*These two steps are important but not essential.

Set the timer one minute for each year of your child's age. Always use a portable timer. The basic steps for using time-out are discussed in *SOS! Help For Parents.*

Methods Of Mild Punishment—Comparison For Parents

Method of Mild Punishment		Age of Child	Effectiveness of Punishment	Type of Behaviors Punished	How Quickly Applied
	Time-Out	Two through Twelve	Extremely effective	Most behavior, especially hard-to-handle behavior	Immediately, if possible
	Scolding and Disapproval	All Ages	Moderately effective	All Behavior	Immediately or later
	Natural Conse-quences	All Ages	Effective	Some Behavior	Immediately or later
"I'm putting your crayons up for ONE WEEK!"	Logical Conse-quences	Three through Adolescence	Effective	Most Behavior	Immediately or later
"Kids don't like it when I tattle." "Kids don't like it when I tattle." "Kids don't like it when I . . . ."	Behavior Penalty	Five through Adolescence	Effective	All Behavior	Immediately or later

Basic Steps For Handling Aggressive
Or Dangerous Behavior—
Parents' Check List

		Immediate Steps To Follow:
✔		

_____ 1. Stop the behavior.

_____ 2. Deliver a brief scolding and name the unacceptable behavior.

_____ *3. Deliver three swats to his bottom (if he is six or younger).

_____ 4. Place him in time-out immediately.

After Time-Out Is Over:

_____ 5. Ask him to say what he did that was aggressive or dangerous.

_____ 6. Help him describe one or two other ways of behaving safely or nonaggressively in the future. Reward him with your praise after he tells you about these other ways of safely behaving.

_____ **7. Follow through with a *mild* logical consequence or behavior penalty. (See Chapter 5)

_____ 8. Use reflective listening *if* your child is in the mood to talk. (Chapter 18)

*You may decide that this step is unnecessary, especially if your child's misbehavior isn't serious or if you oppose the use of "swats."
**This step may be unnecessary also, depending on the seriousness of your child's behavior.

Chapter 17 of *SOS! Help For Parents* discusses the basic steps for handling aggressive or dangerous behavior.

Point-Reward Calendar
For Improving *One* Behavior

POINTS EARNED							
Good Behavior (and possible points):							
	S	**M**	**T**	**W**	**T**	**F**	**S**
First Week							
Second Week							
Third Week							

This calendar records *one* behavior for *several weeks.* At the end of the third week, post a new calendar.

When your child spends a point, draw a red mark or slash through that point. Points without slash marks are points not yet spent. Encourage your child to spend her points rather than save them. Chapter 14 of *SOS! Help For Parents* describes how to use a point-reward calendar to improve behavior.

Point-Reward Calendar
For Improving *Several* Behaviors

POINTS EARNED

List of Good Behaviors (and possible points)	S	M	T	W	T	F	S
TOTAL POINTS EARNED							

This calendar provides a record of *several* behaviors for *one week.* Post a new calendar each week.

At the end of each day, total the number of points your child has earned. Draw marks through points on the bottom line when your child spends those points. Chapter 14 of *SOS! Help For Parents* describes how to use a point-reward calendar to improve behavior.

Menu of Rewards

Menu of Rewards	
Reward	**Cost in Points**

List material rewards and activity rewards on this menu. Also list the number of points (or tokens) that your child must pay for each reward. Post this menu next to the point-reward calendar.

Chapter 14 of *SOS! Help For Parents* describes how to use a menu of rewards to improve behavior.

Parent-Child Contract Form

CONTRACT

I, _____, agree to: _____
(child's name)

_____

_____

_____

_____

We, Mother and Father, agree to: _____

_____

_____

_____

_____

Date contract begins: _____

Date contract ends: _____

Date contract signed: _____

Agreed to by: _____
                             (Child's signature)

                             _____
                             (Mother)

                             _____
                             (Father)

Chapter 14 of *SOS! Help For Parents* describes how to use parent-child contracts.

Parent-Teacher-Child Record Form

Record of _____ Target Behavior
(child's name)

Week of: _____

	M	T	W	T	F
Target behavior: _____ _____ (teacher records each day)					
Teacher's initials: (teacher signs each day)					
Child's initials: (child signs each day)					
Parent's initials: (parent signs each evening)					

Plan: _____

_____

_____

_____

Chapter 20 of *SOS! Help For Parents* describes how to use parent-teacher-child record forms.

Information For Parents

"All I did was HIT Jonathan once!"

Dear Parents,

All classrooms have behavior problems from time to time. TIME-OUT is a safe, nonaggressive way for helping children to improve their behavior. Time-out is placing a child in a dull, boring place for a brief period of time following the child's misbehavior.

Time-out is used for hitting, kicking, shoving, scratching, biting, spitting at others, behavior dangerous to oneself, and threatening others. Sometimes children are placed in time-out for grabbing things from others, repeatedly disobeying classroom rules, swearing, angry screeching, and sassy talk to me.

Normally, you shouldn't punish your child at home if you find out that he was placed in time-out at school. You want your child to feel free to tell you about what is happening at school!

Time-out can also be used to help correct a child's misbehavior at home. Please ask me any questions that you may have about time-out or other methods that I use to help children.

_____
(teacher)

The Video SOS! Help For Parents

A Video-Discussion

Parent Education

Program

   This video parent education program is based on the book, SOS! Help For Parents. It includes the 55 minute VHS videocassette, Video Leader's Guide, parent handouts, and SOS! Help For Parents book.

   It is used by counselors, parent groups, educators, churches, and social service professionals and is intended for parenting workshops, staff development, in-service training, teacher training, and classroom use.

   Part One may be viewed by a group or individually. For Part Two, a group leader familiar with SOS needs to guide the discussion following each of the parenting scenes. The easy-to-use Video Leader's Guide offers discussion questions for each scene. The SOS Sampler-Preview Video demonstrates how you can use The SOS Video to educate others in SOS parenting skills and methods. The SOS Video is enjoyable and user-friendly!

SOS! Help For Professionals
A kit of parent education and counseling materials
(See page 209)

   The SOS! Help For Professionals kit includes the following: (1) SOS! Help For Parents book, (2) How To Use Time-Out Effectively audiotape, (3) Child Rearing Methods flip cards, (4) Time-Out Steps flip cards, (5) Time-Out Parent Inventory, (6) Parent Handouts, (7) Quizzes for parents, (8) Professional Manual, & (9) other materials. Professionals educating or counseling parents will find the SOS! Help For Professionals kit useful.

How To Use Time-Out Effectively
Audiotape (67 minutes).
   This audiotape demonstrates and teaches time-out skills. Time-out is demonstrated with a young child. Also, two older children tell how they feel about time-out. You'll hear answers to common time-out questions and learn to avoid nine common time-out mistakes. The audiotape includes "time-out for two" and "time-out for toys" and is suitable for individual or group listening.

Parents Press
Post Office Box 2180, Bowling Green, KY 42102

SOS books <u>cannot</u> be ordered through bookstores.
Conveniently order SOS books and materials from the Publisher.

_____ Copies of **SOS! Help For Parents** book for $9.95 plus $1.50 shipping. (Book ISBN 0-935111-16-6)

_____ Copies of **How To Use Time-Out Effectively** audiotape (67 minutes) for $9.50 plus $1.50 shipping. (Audiotape ISBN 0-935111-32-8) See page 242.

_____ **SOS! Help For Professionals** kit for $45.95 plus $3.00 shipping. For counselors, educators, and social service professionals. Includes SOS! Help For Parents book, How To Use Time-Out Effectively audiotape, flip cards, & other materials. (Kit ISBN 0-935111-24-7) See pp. 209 & 242.

_____ **SOS Sampler-Preview Video** for $12.00, shipping included. This $12.00 can be applied later to the price of the full SOS Video described below. (Sampler-Preview Video ISBN 0-935111-37-9)

_____ **The Video SOS! Help For Parents** education program for $150.00, shipping included. The SOS Video is used by counselors, parent groups, educators, churches, and social service professionals. Program includes 55 minute videocassette, Video Leader's Guide, parent handouts, and SOS! Help For Parents book. (SOS Video ISBN 0-935111-44-1) See page 242.

If not satisfied, I understand that I may return any of the materials for a refund, except The SOS Video. Orders from individuals must be prepaid by check or money order. Agency purchase orders are accepted. Telephone orders are not possible at this time. Federal ID No. 510361116.

Mailing Label -- Please Print

Name: _____	
Address: _____	
City: _____ State: _____ Zip: _____	

Shipping: Include only $1.50 for first SOS book or SOS audiotape and .50¢ for each additional book or audiotape.

Quantity Discounts: If you are ordering at least five books and/or audiotapes, deduct 20% from the cost of your order.

____ I can't wait 3 weeks for Book Rate. Enclosed is $2.50 total shipping per book or audiotape for air mail.

____ I am a professional working with parents and/or children. Please send a professionals' SOS Catalog of parent education materials.

Foreign country orders: All orders must be prepaid in US funds (money orders, checks on US banks). For foreign shipping, double US shipping rates. The SOS! Help For Professionals kit is too heavy to ship by air mail. It is shipped to foreign countries only by Surface Book Rate.

The Video SOS! Help For Parents

A Video-Discussion

Parent Education

Program

This video parent education program is based on the book, SOS! Help For Parents. It includes the 55 minute VHS videocassette, Video Leader's Guide, parent handouts, and SOS! Help For Parents book.

It is used by counselors, parent groups, educators, churches, and social service professionals and is intended for parenting workshops, staff development, in-service training, teacher training, and classroom use.

Part One may be viewed by a group or individually. For Part Two, a group leader familiar with SOS needs to guide the discussion following each of the parenting scenes. The easy-to-use Video Leader's Guide offers discussion questions for each scene. The SOS Sampler-Preview Video demonstrates how you can use The SOS Video to educate others in SOS parenting skills and methods. The SOS Video is enjoyable and user-friendly!

SOS! Help For Professionals
A kit of parent education and counseling materials
(See page 209)

The SOS! Help For Professionals kit includes the following: (1) SOS! Help For Parents book, (2) How To Use Time-Out Effectively audiotape, (3) Child Rearing Methods flip cards, (4) Time-Out Steps flip cards, (5) Time-Out Parent Inventory, (6) Parent Handouts, (7) Quizzes for parents, (8) Professional Manual, & (9) other materials. Professionals educating or counseling parents will find the SOS! Help For Professionals kit useful.

How To Use Time-Out Effectively
Audiotape (67 minutes).

This audiotape demonstrates and teaches time-out skills. Time-out is demonstrated with a young child. Also, two older children tell how they feel about time-out. You'll hear answers to common time-out questions and learn to avoid nine common time-out mistakes. The audiotape includes "time-out for two" and "time-out for toys" and is suitable for individual or group listening.

Parents Press
Post Office Box 2180, Bowling Green, KY 42102

SOS books cannot be ordered through bookstores.
Conveniently order SOS books and materials from the Publisher.

_____ Copies of **SOS! Help For Parents** book for $9.95 plus $1.50 shipping. (Book ISBN 0-935111-16-6)

_____ Copies of **How To Use Time-Out Effectively** audiotape (67 minutes) for $9.50 plus $1.50 shipping. (Audiotape ISBN 0-935111-32-8) See page 242.

_____ **SOS! Help For Professionals** kit for $45.95 plus $3.00 shipping. For counselors, educators, and social service professionals. Includes SOS! Help For Parents book, How To Use Time-Out Effectively audiotape, flip cards, & other materials. (Kit ISBN 0-935111-24-7) See pp. 209 & 242.

_____ **SOS Sampler-Preview Video** for $12.00, shipping included. This $12.00 can be applied later to the price of the full SOS Video described below. (Sampler-Preview Video ISBN 0-935111-37-9)

_____ **The Video SOS! Help For Parents** education program for $150.00, shipping included. The SOS Video is used by counselors, parent groups, educators, churches, and social service professionals. Program includes 55 minute videocassette, Video Leader's Guide, parent handouts, and SOS! Help For Parents book. (SOS Video ISBN 0-935111-44-1) See page 242.

If not satisfied, I understand that I may return any of the materials for a refund, except The SOS Video. Orders from individuals must be prepaid by check or money order. Agency purchase orders are accepted. Telephone orders are not possible at this time. Federal ID No. 510361116.

Mailing Label -- Please Print

Name: _____

Address: _____

City: _____ State: _____ Zip: _____

Shipping: Include only $1.50 for first SOS book or SOS audiotape and .50¢ for each additional book or audiotape.

Quantity Discounts: If you are ordering at least five books and/or audiotapes, deduct 20% from the cost of your order.

_____ I can't wait 3 weeks for Book Rate. Enclosed is $2.50 total shipping per book or audiotape for air mail.

_____ I am a professional working with parents and/or children. Please send a professionals' SOS Catalog of parent education materials.

Foreign country orders: All orders must be prepaid in US funds (money orders, checks on US banks). For foreign shipping, double US shipping rates. The SOS! Help For Professionals kit is too heavy to ship by air mail. It is shipped to foreign countries only by Surface Book Rate.

The Video SOS! Help For Parents

A Video-Discussion

Parent Education

Program

   This video parent education program is based on the book, SOS! Help For Parents. It includes the 55 minute VHS videocassette, Video Leader's Guide, parent handouts, and SOS! Help For Parents book.

   It is used by counselors, parent groups, educators, churches, and social service professionals and is intended for parenting workshops, staff development, in-service training, teacher training, and classroom use.

   Part One may be viewed by a group or individually. For Part Two, a group leader familiar with SOS needs to guide the discussion following each of the parenting scenes. The easy-to-use Video Leader's Guide offers discussion questions for each scene. The SOS Sampler-Preview Video demonstrates how <u>you</u> can use The SOS Video to educate others in SOS parenting skills and methods. The SOS Video is enjoyable and user-friendly!

SOS! Help For Professionals
A kit of parent education and
counseling materials
(See page 209)

   The SOS! Help For Professionals kit includes the following: (1) SOS! Help For Parents book, (2) How To Use Time-Out Effectively audiotape, (3) Child Rearing Methods flip cards, (4) Time-Out Steps flip cards, (5) Time-Out Parent Inventory, (6) Parent Handouts, (7) Quizzes for parents, (8) Professional Manual, & (9) other materials. Professionals educating or counseling parents will find the SOS! Help For Professionals kit useful.

How To Use Time-Out Effectively
Audiotape (67 minutes).
   This audiotape demonstrates and teaches time-out skills. Time-out is demonstrated with a young child. Also, two older children tell how they feel about time-out. You'll hear answers to common time-out questions and learn to avoid nine common time-out mistakes. The audiotape includes "time-out for two" and "time-out for toys" and is suitable for individual or group listening.